LIST OF CONTENTS

All photoplates courtesy of RAC Museum

COVER: 75mm GMC M3

INTRODUCTION

In accordance with the established practice of the Datafile Series, this book concentrates on the organisation, disposition and markings of Tank Destroyer units. It is felt necessary to add some background on the tactics and organisation of these units in order to clarify the reasons for change. It is considered beyond the scope of this volume to enter into either combat history or tactical philosophy, both of which are covered by other works.

Because of the predominance of battalion size units in the Tank Destroyer Force it has been possible to explore the establishment tables, personnel and equipment, in some detail, which enables the development of these features between 1941 and 1945 to be appreciated. These establishments record the official allocation of men & vehicles, though it must be stressed that these allocations were often modified in the field to match availability. In some cases vehicles are specified in anticipation of their introduction, which was either delayed or cancelled after development work was completed. Similarly some vehicles, such as the M36, were already in action before appearing in the T/O & E's. These table must not, therefore, be taken as absolute.

The Tank Destroyer Field Manual specifying the tactical doctrine appears to have be conceived at the time of the axis armored blitzkreig (1939-40) and although some modifications were made later, the basic concept does not change significantly despite the changes to armored warfare. Again, battalions were converted to towed guns for concealment following desert experience in North Africa just as the Armies moved into the more populated areas of Europe, and both allied and enemy commands were moving from towed to self-propelled anti-tank guns. These facts would tend to indicate a decided lack of communication or response between command and field units.

Three powers developed the tank destroyer concept during the war, these being the Soviet Army (SU-85, SU-100), the German Army (Jagdpanzer Hetzer, Mk IV and JagdPanther) and the US Army (described herein). The main difference in equipment was that Soviet and German Tank Destroyers as indicated above were armored, and even took the place of tank battalions, whilst US Tank Destroyers were only very lightly armored with crews vulnerable to shrapnel, grenades and HE in the open gun compartments. A unique feature of the US doctrine was that all heavy anti-tank artillery was grouped in the Tank Destroyer Battalions, leaving the organic divisional anti-tank units with the less than effective 37mm (later 57mm) towed guns.

The demise of the US Tank Destroyer battalions was almost as sudden as their appearance. By 1944 the superiority of the Tank Destroyer guns over the contemporary US tanks began to disappear, and by the end of the war the tank had taken over all the duties of the Tank Destroyer. It may therefore be concluded that for a considerable period, the guns of the Tank Destroyers had filled a gap which might otherwise have proved at least an embarrassment to US Forces in the field.

£5.75 NN

U.S. Tank Destroyers
of World War Two

Compiled and published by:-

Mr. MALCOLM A. BELLIS
10 WHITE HART LANE
WISTASTON, CREWE

M10A1 3-inch GMC
(1:76 scale Cromwell
Models)

(Author)

M6 Dodge 4x4 37mm
(1:72 scale ESCI)

(Author)

TANK DESTROYER TACTICS - THEORY & PRACTICE

When the German blitzkreig of 1939-40 overcame Polish, French and British regular forces in a matter of days from the outset of a campaign, the US Army abruptly became aware of the total lack of counter measures to this type of warfare. At that time US armour comprised about 400 light tanks with a few medium tanks. Anti-tank artillery relied on the 37mm gun copied from the German PaK 36 and the 75mm field gun adopted from the French in 1917.

Against this background the 'Tank Destroyer' philosophy came into being, lightly-armored guns at battalion strength acting as a semi-independent mobile reserve and striking enemy armor in rapidly developed attacks from front and flank. Prescribed in the Tank Destroyer Field Manual FM 18-5, reflected in the Force motto 'Seek, Strike and Destroy', this aggressive philosophy was virtually unchanged throughout the war years.

First taking the field in North Africa, the Tank destroyer battalions scored some victories and suffered some defeats. The most obvious fact to emerge from these engagements was that in 1943 axis armor did not use the same tactics they had used in 1940, having had wider experience in the Western Desert and the Russian Front. The TD battalions, trained to combat an attack which rarely materialised, remained in the rear of the field troops armed, fuelled and impotent. This did not suit the field commanders, who resented the waste of men and equipment, and began to adversely affect the morale of the crews themselves. The battalions, and sometimes individual companies, were increasingly attached to the field forces, usually at divisional level. As the war progressed into Italy, periods of attachment became prolonged, although the TD units never adopted the insignia or markings of the units with which they served.

Amongst the first techniques developed was indirect fire, a Tank Destroyer Gun Company divided into two batteries of six guns complementing the 105mm howitzers of the Divisional Field Artillery. The three-inch guns with range up to 14,000 yards were used for long-range harassment whilst the heavier 105mm howitzers worked within their 10,000 yard range. In the 'static' phases of the Italian Campaign, dug-in Tank Destroyers might be employed in this role for several weeks.

It was discovered that the tank destroyer guns were very effective against concrete emplacements. Specially trained crews were required to place a 3-inch round through the embrasure of an enemy pillbox at 1500 yards. For particularly difficult bunkers, all four guns of a platoon would be fired at the target simultaneously for maximum effect. Stalking to the rear of a pillbox, firing one round at the door and a second through the doorway was also used. The 90mm gun fitted to the M36 was capable of penetrating 4.5 feet of unreinforced concrete.

In the primary role against tanks some of the best results were obtained when poor visibility aided stalking. This is evident from actions at Arracourt, September 1944 when 704th Bn claimed 15 enemy tanks for loss of four M18's and at Elsenborn in December 1944 when 644th Bn claimed 17 for the loss of two M10's. For the 3-inch gun to penetrate frontal armour of a Tiger, the range was estimated as 50 yards in practice (ordnance optimistically stated 2000 yards). Only the 90mm M36 was considered an even match for later axis medium and heavy tanks, a record existing of an M36 claiming a Panther kill at 3,200 yards.

TANK DESTROYER ORGANISATION

In 1937, field trials with the three-regiment (triangular) infantry division led to recommendations that each division should be allocated a battalion of 24 anti-tank guns and each infantry regiment within the division a company of 14 anti-tank guns. These proposals were implemented in 1939-40.

Experimental formations of lightly armored, mobile anti-tank guns were employed in an aggressive role during the 1941 Army Maneuvers, the results being claimed as justification for the 'Tank Destroyer' doctrine. To avoid rival claims for parentage from different arms of service, which had bedevilled the introduction of armored units, the Tank Destroyers were placed under direct command of GHQ. The anti-tank battalions allocated to infantry divisions were withdrawn to assist in the formation of the new Tank Destroyer battalions.

The first tables of organisation were issued in December 1941 prescribing two types of battalion, 'Light' & 'Heavy'. Some 53 battalions were formed to these requirements, the type of formation no doubt being governed by availability of equipment as much as tactical considerations. New tables issued in June 1942 were based on the 'Heavy' battalion, the prefix 'Light' or 'Heavy' being deleted. Units entering combat in North Africa were based on the June 1942 type organisation. In November 1942 the Light Company in the battalion was replaced by a (third) Heavy Company.

The organisation specified in the January 1943 tables rationalised the administrative and support troops, released the AA sections to Corps Troops and reduced personnel from 898 to 673 whilst retaining its complement of 36 guns. For the first time a single type of gun was specified, the 3-inch anti-tank self-propelled. There was no further significant change to the organisation of the SP battalions, the main differences in later tables being related to equipment and technical skills.

The difficulty in concealing self-propelled tank destroyers during the North African Campaign led to the introduction of the towed 3-inch gun battalion. The tables issued in May 1943 specified 816 personnel, the towed guns requiring a crew of ten. To facilitate the extra manpower, the Reconnaissance Company was replaced by two platoons within the Headquarters Company. The towed guns proved difficult to move and were less versatile than the SP guns. In Normandy towed battalions accounted for about 20% of the tank destroyer 'kills', whilst 65 of the 77 tank destroyers lost by First Army in the Ardennes were towed guns. Most towed battalions had been converted back to SP units by early 1945

The Tank Destroyer Group, of which 24 were formed, was intended as the command module for the battalions containing a Headquarters and Headquarters Company without guns. The battalions became so dispersed that in practice the Group functioned in a mainly administrative capacity at Corps level.

The Tank Destroyer Force reached a peak of 106 battalions in late 1943, when it was decided that this number could not be usefully employed in the Tank Destroyer role. In the following months some 28 battalions were either disbanded and personnel utilised elsewhere or were converted to other roles e.g. amphibious tractor battalions.

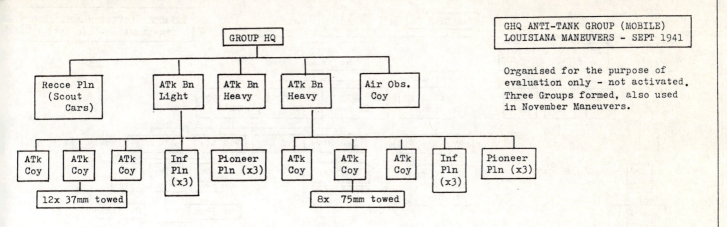

GHQ ANTI-TANK GROUP (MOBILE)
LOUISIANA MANEUVERS - SEPT 1941

Organised for the purpose of
evaluation only - not activated.
Three Groups formed, also used
in November Maneuvers.

GROUP HQ

Recce Pln
(Scout
Cars)

ATk Bn
Light

ATk Bn
Heavy

ATk Bn
Heavy

Air Obs.
Coy

ATk Coy

ATk Coy

ATk Coy

Inf Pln (x3)

Pioneer Pln (x3)

ATk Coy

ATk Coy

ATk Coy

Inf Pln (x3)

Pioneer Pln (x3)

12x 37mm towed

8x 75mm towed

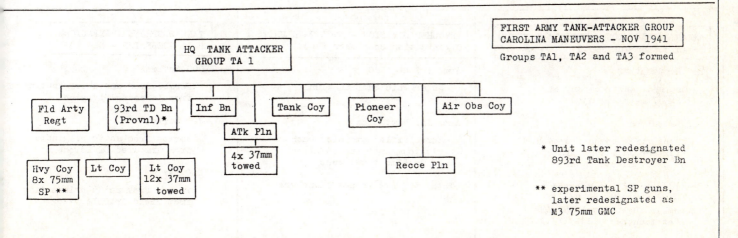

FIRST ARMY TANK-ATTACKER GROUP
CAROLINA MANEUVERS - NOV 1941

Groups TA1, TA2 and TA3 formed

HQ TANK ATTACKER
GROUP TA 1

Fld Arty
Regt

93rd TD Bn
(Provnl)*

Inf Bn

Tank Coy

Pioneer
Coy

Air Obs Coy

ATk Pln

4x 37mm
towed

Recce Pln

Hvy Coy
8x 75mm
SP **

Lt Coy

Lt Coy
12x 37mm
towed

* Unit later redesignated
893rd Tank Destroyer Bn

** experimental SP guns,
later redesignated as
M3 75mm GMC

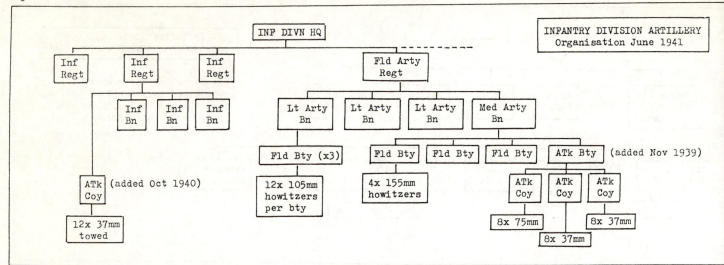

INFANTRY DIVISION ARTILLERY
Organisation June 1941

INF DIVN HQ

Inf Regt · Inf Regt · Inf Regt · Fld Arty Regt

Inf Bn · Inf Bn · Inf Bn

Lt Arty Bn · Lt Arty Bn · Lt Arty Bn · Med Arty Bn

ATk Coy (added Oct 1940)

Fld Bty (x3)

Fld Bty · Fld Bty · Fld Bty · ATk Bty (added Nov 1939)

12x 37mm towed

12x 105mm howitzers per bty

4x 155mm howitzers

ATk Coy · ATk Coy · ATk Coy

8x 75mm · 8x 37mm

8x 37mm

INFANTRY DIVISION - ANTI TANK UNITS
Organisation July 1943

Inf Regiment HQ

    One anti tank company of 12x 57mm towed guns

Inf Battalion

    Three rifle companies each with one anti tank platoon of 3x 57mm towed guns

Anti tank battery deleted to form Tank Destroyer Bns, December 1941. Total 557 ATk rocket launchers, July 1943

ARMOURED DIVISION - ANTI TANK UNITS
Organisation September 1943

Armd Inf Regt HQ

    No organic anti tank unit

Armd Inf Battalion

    Three rifle companies each with one anti tank platoon of 3x 57mm towed guns

Total 607 ATk rocket launchers

TANK DESTROYER BATTALIONS
UNIT NUMBERING - Dec 1941

600 Series

    Formed from units originating from Infantry Divisions

700 Series

    Formed from units originating from Armoured Divisions

800 Series

    Formed from units originating from Field Artillery Regts

HISTORICAL SUMMARY

Bde	Formed	History	Inactivated
1st	11.42	UK (1.44), N.Fr (7.44), Task Force 'A', Brittany (8.44), TD Section-3rd Army (10.44)	Germany 10.45
2nd	11.42	USA only, TD Center Bde,(11.42), 2nd Army (4.43), XX Corps (11.43)	USA 3.44

Grp	Formed	History	Inactivated
1	3.42	UK (8.42), N.Af (1.43), It (10.43), UK (12.43), N.Fr (6.44) as VII Cps Traffic Cont Sec	Germany 11.45
2	3.42	UK (1.44), N.Fr (6.44) as XIX Cps anti-tank section	Germany 11.45
3	3.42	UK (11.43), N.Fr (6.44) as V Cps anti-tank section, returned USA Feb 1946	USA 2.46
4	9.42	UK (4.44), N.Fr (7.44) as XX Cps anti-tank section, returned USA July 1945	USA 10.45
5	9.42	UK (1.44), N.Fr (7.44) as XV Cps anti-tank section, returned USA Dec 1945	USA 12.45
6	9.42	UK (2.44), N.Fr (7.44) as XIII Cps anti-tank section, redes 5 Constabulary Regt	Germany 5.46
7	9.42	UK (2.44), N.Fr (7.44) as VIII Cps anti-tank section,	Germany 3.46
8	10.42	UK (9.44), N.Fr (10.44) as III Cps anti-tank section, returned USA July 1945	USA 10.45
9	10.42	UK (5.44), N.Fr (7.44) as XII Cps Advanced Information Ctr, returned USA Aug 1945	USA 11.45
10	2.43	USA only, attached 3rd Army, X Cps, Desert Training Ctr, III Cps then XXIII Cps	USA 5.44
11	2.43	USA only, attached 3rd Army, VIII Cps, XVIII Cps then XXIII Cps	USA 5.44
12	2.43	UK (9.44), N.Fr (10.44) as XVI Cps anti-tank section, returned USA June 1945	USA 11.45
13	3.43	Hawaii (1.45), Leyte (7.45), Mindoro, Philippines (8.45)	Mindoro 11.45
14	3.43	USA only, attached XI Cps, 2nd Army, XX Cps then XXII Cps	USA 5.44
15	3.43	USA only, attached II Armd Cps, XVI Cps then XXXVI Cps	USA 8.44
16	4.43	UK (11.44), N.Fr (2.45) as XXI Cps anti-tank section, returned USA Sept 1945	USA 11.45
17	4.43	USA only, attached VIII Cps, XVIII Cps then XXIII Cps	USA 8.44
18	4.43	USA only, attached IX Cps, XXI Cps, XXIII Cps then XXI Cps	USA 2.45
19	5.43	USA only, attached XVI Cps, 4th Army then IX Cps	USA 5.44
20	5.43	UK (10.44), N.Fr (10.44) as 9th Army Rear Detatchment, returned USA Sept 1945	USA 11.45
21	5.43	USA only, attached IX Cps	USA 11.45
22	6.43	USA only, assigned Replacement and Command School, Feb 1944	USA 2.45
23	6.43	UK (10.44), N.Fr (10.44), Belgium (11.44), Germany (3.45), returned USA July 1945	USA 10.45
24	6.43	USA only, attached XXIII Cps then 4th Army	USA 12.44

TANK DESTROYER TACTICAL & FIRING CENTER

Activated 27 November 1941, Fort Meade, Maryland. Relocated Camp Hood, Texas, 30 January 1942. Redesignated Tank Destroyer Command, 14 March 1942, reverted to Tank Destroyer Center 17 August 1942. Disbanded 10 November 1945

TANK DESTROYER GROUP - HEADQUARTERS & HQ COMPANY - PERSONNEL

T/O & E 18-10-1 30th December 1943	GROUP HEADQUARTERS		HEADQUARTERS COMPANY		NOTES
	Command Section	Operations Section	Company HQ	Communications Platoon	
Colonel	1	-	-	-	Initial T/O & E dated 5th January 1942 called for 16 officers and 115 enlisted men. This was reduced in December of that year to total 8 officers and 40 other ranks, this being only slightly increased in change dated May 1943.
Lieutenant colonel	1	-	-	-	
Major	3	-	-	-	
Captain	3	-	-	-	
First lieutenant	1	-	-	1	
Second lieutenant	-	-	-	-	
:armed Pistol .45cal	9	-	1	1	
					This page shows the personnel called for
Warrant officer	-	-	-	-	This was used during the North African and Italian Campaigns and was the subject of only minor revisions to personnel in later changes.
Master sergeant	-	2	-	1	
First sergeant	-	-	1	-	
Technical sergeant	-	1	-	-	
Staff sergeant	-	-	2	1	
:armed Pistol .45cal	-	3	3	2	
Sergeant	-	1	1	-	The table of vehicles opposite shows change to vehicle type and armament, little change being made to the number of vehicles.
Corporal	-	-	1	1	
:armed Carbine .3cal	-	-	2	1	
Other ranks	-	9	19	17	A small section for chaplains & medical were included.
:armed Carbine .3cal	-	9	19	17	

TANK DESTROYER GROUP - VEHICLES

T/O & E 18-10-1 26th May 1943 (1st table) 30th Dec 1943 31st Oct 1944 (2nd table)	HEADQUARTERS & HQ COMPANY						REMARKS
	Group HQ		HQ Coy		(attached)		
	Commd	Opns	HQ	Comms	Chaplain	Medic	
Car, Armd, Utility, M10	-	-	-	3	-	-	Subs Veh Half-Track M2
Motorcycle - solo	-	-	-	2	-	-	
Truck:							
¼ton 4x4 (jeep)	-	-	-	3	1-2	-	one per chaplain
¾ton Command	-	-	-	1	-	-	
¾ton Weapons Carrier	-	-	2**[1]	-	-	-	
1½ton 6x6 Cargo	-	-	1	-	-	-	
Trailers:							
¼ton, 2whl, cargo	-	-	2	1	1-2	-	* with .3cal MG ** with .5cal MG
1ton, 2whl, cargo	-	-	1	-	-	-	
Launcher, rocket, 2.36in	-	-	5	-	-	-	
Car, Armd, Utility, M20	-	2**	-	-	-	-	Subs Veh Half-Track M2
Car, Half-Track, M3A2	-	2**[1]	-	1*	-	-	
Truck:							
¼ton 4x4 (jeep)	-	-	-	4*[1]	2	1	rep by ¾ton Wpns Carrier, 2.44
¾ton Command	-	-	-	1	-	-	
¾ton Weapons Carrier	-	-	1	-	-	-	
1½ton 6x6 Cargo	-	-	1	-	-	-	
2½ton 6x6 Cargo	-	-	1**[1]	-	-	-	n.b. Armd Utility M10 redesignated M20
Trailers:							
¼ton, 2whl, cargo	-	-	-	-	2	1	
1ton, 2whl, cargo	-	-	2	1	-	-	
Launcher, rocket, 2.36in	-	-	5	-	-	-	

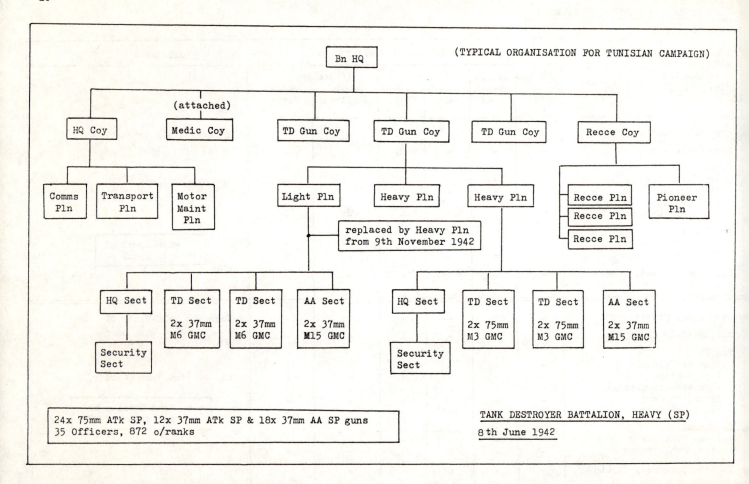

(TYPICAL ORGANISATION FOR TUNISIAN CAMPAIGN)

Bn HQ

(attached)

HQ Coy | Medic Coy | TD Gun Coy | TD Gun Coy | TD Gun Coy | Recce Coy

Comms Pln | Transport Pln | Motor Maint Pln

Light Pln | Heavy Pln | Heavy Pln

Recce Pln | Recce Pln | Recce Pln | Pioneer Pln

replaced by Heavy Pln from 9th November 1942

HQ Sect

Security Sect

TD Sect
2x 37mm M6 GMC

TD Sect
2x 37mm M6 GMC

AA Sect
2x 37mm M15 GMC

HQ Sect

Security Sect

TD Sect
2x 75mm M3 GMC

TD Sect
2x 75mm M3 GMC

AA Sect
2x 37mm M15 GMC

24x 75mm ATk SP, 12x 37mm ATk SP & 18x 37mm AA SP guns
35 Officers, 872 o/ranks

TANK DESTROYER BATTALION, HEAVY (SP)

8th June 1942

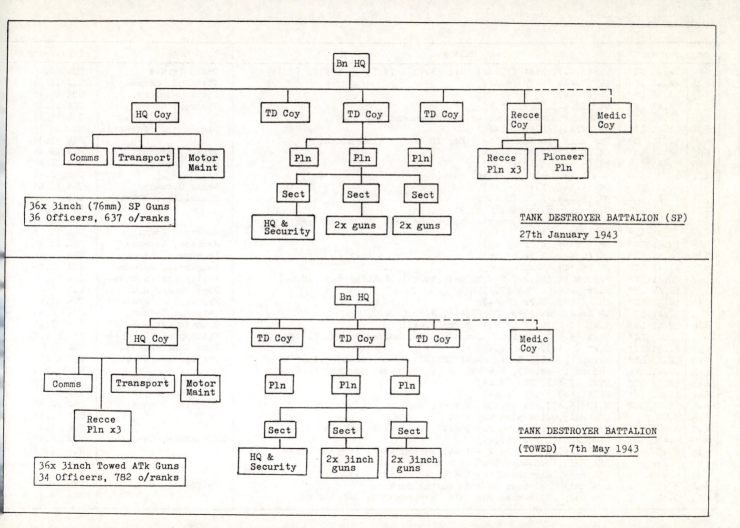

Bn HQ

HQ Coy — Comms, Transport, Motor Maint

TD Coy, TD Coy, TD Coy

Pln, Pln, Pln

Sect — HQ & Security

Sect — 2x guns

Sect — 2x guns

Recce Coy — Recce Pln x3, Pioneer Pln

Medic Coy

36x 3inch (76mm) SP Guns
36 Officers, 637 o/ranks

TANK DESTROYER BATTALION (SP)
27th January 1943

Bn HQ

HQ Coy — Comms, Recce Pln x3, Transport, Motor Maint

TD Coy, TD Coy, TD Coy

Pln, Pln, Pln

Sect — HQ & Security

Sect — 2x 3inch guns

Sect — 2x 3inch guns

Medic Coy

36x 3inch Towed ATk Guns
34 Officers, 782 o/ranks

TANK DESTROYER BATTALION
(TOWED) 7th May 1943

Bn	Formed	History	Locn 8.45	Inactivated
601	12.41 LT*	UK (8.42), N.Af (11.42), Sic (7.43), It (9.43), N.Fr (8.44)	Toul, France	USA 10.45
602	12.41 LT*	UK (7.44), N.Fr (8.44),	Wittlich, Germany	USA 11.45
603	12.41 LT*	UK (4.44), N.Fr (7.44),	Chateau-Salins, Fr	USA 12.45
605	12.41 LT*	UK (12.44), N.Fr (1.45),	Viersen, Germany	USA 11.45
606	12.41 LT*	USA only, transferred to R & S Command Nov 1944		USA 2.45
607	12.41 LT*	UK (4.44), N.Fr (6.44),	Lissendorf, Germany	USA 10.45
608	12.41 LT*	USA only, personnel to other TD Bns on disbandment		USA 11.43
609	12.41 LT*	UK (8.44), N.Fr (9.44),	Trier, Germany	USA 11.45
610	4.42	UK (6.44), N.Fr (8.44),	Prum, Germany	USA 12.45
611	5.42 T	USA only, retained towed guns,		USA 2.45
612	6.42	UK (4.44), N.Fr (6.44),	Bonn, Germany	USA 10.45
614	7.42	UK (9.44), N.Fr (9.44),	Bouxwiller, France	USA 1.46
626	12.41 LT*	USA only, disbanded Dec 1943		USA 12.43
627	12.41 LT*	Hawaii (7.42), converted to provisional QM Bn Jan 1945		Hawaii 4.45
628	12.41 LT*	UK (2.44), N.Fr (7.44),	Neersen, Germany	USA 11.45
629	12.41 LT*	UK (1.44), N.Fr (7.44),	Neurath, Germany	USA 12.45
630	12.41 LT*	UK (6.44), N.Fr (7.44),	Iversheim, Germany	USA 3.46
631	12.41 LT*	UK (8.44), N.Fr (8.44),	Langgreis, Germany	USA 12.45
632	12.41 LT*	Australia (5.42), New Guinea (10.43), Philippines (10.44)	Philippine Islands	USA 1.46
633	12.41 LT*	N.Fr (4.45), USA 7.45)	Fort Bragg, N.C.	USA 10.45
634	12.41 LT*	UK (1.44), N.Fr (6.44),	Versailles, France	USA 11.45
635	12.41 LT	SP from June 1943, UK (2.44), N.Fr (7.44),	Leipzig, Germany	USA 12.45
636	12.41 LT*	N.Af (4.43), It (9.43), N.Fr (8.44),	Brumath, France	USA 12.45
637	12.41 LT*	Fiji (6.42), Espiritu Santo (7.44), Bourgainville (10.44)	Philippines (1.45+)	Japan 1.46
638	12.41 LT*	N.Fr (9.44), USA (7.45)	Fort Benning, Ga.	USA 11.45
640	12.41 LT*	Hawaii (9.42), Guadalcanal (2.44), New Britain (5.44)	Philippines (1.45+)	USA 1.46
641	12.41 LT	Australia (4.42), New Guinea (1.43) redes 98 Chem Mort Bn		NGuin 6.44
643	12.41 LT*	N.Fr (9.44), USA (7.45),	Cp San Luis Obispo	USA 11.45
644	12.41 LT*	UK (1.44), N.Fr (7.44),	Bergerhausen, Ger.	USA 12.45
645	12.41 LSP	N.Af (5.43), It (9.43), N.Fr (8.44)	Hambach, France	USA 10.45
646	5.42	USA only, disbanded May 1944		USA 5.44
647	3.43	USA only, disbanded May 1944, personnel to 144 Inf Bn		USA 5.44
648	3.43	UK (12.44), N.Fr (1.45)	Schwabach, Germany	USA 12.45
649	3.43	USA only, disbanded Apr 1944, personnel to Army Services		USA 5.44
650	3.43	USA only, redesignated 425th Armd Fld Arty Bn Mar 1944		USA 3.44
651	3.43	USA only, disbabded May 1944, personnel to 140 Inf Bn		USA 5.44
652	3.43	USA only, retained SP guns during service	Cp Shelby, Miss	USA 9.45
653	3.43	USA only, disbanded May 1944, personnel to 144 Inf Bn		USA 5.44

HISTORICAL SUMMARY

Bn	Formed	History	Locn 8.45	Inactivated
654	12.41 LSP	UK (10.43), N.Fr (7.44),	Venlo, Holland	USA 11.45
655	4.43	USA only, disbanded 4.44, personnel to 493 & 869 Ord Maint Coys		USA 4.44
656	3.43	UK (12.44), N.Fr (2.45), USA (7.45)	Cp Campbell, Ken'tky	USA 11.46
657	4.43	USA only, disbanded 4.44, personnel to 493 & 869 Ord Maint Coys		USA 4.44
658	4.43	USA only, redesignated 658 Amphibious Tractor Bn, Apr 1944		USA 4.44
659	5.43 T	USA only, Towed Guns, to R & S Command Nov 1944		USA 11.44
660	4.43	USA only, TD School Tps 5.43, R & S Commd,- pers to 201 Inf Bn		USA 5.44
661	4.43	N.Fr (1.45), USA (7.45)	Cp Shelby, Miss.	USA 2.46
662	5.43 T	USA only, R & S Commd Feb 1944, redes. 662 Tank Bn Dec 1944		USA 12.44
663	5.43	USA only, redesignated 426 Armd Fld Arty Bn, Mar 1944		USA 3.44
664	5.43	USA only, disbanded May 1944, personnel to 125 Inf Bn		USA 5.44
665	5.43	USA only, disbanded May 1944, personnel to 125 Inf Bn		USA 5.44
666	5.43	USA only, redesignated 427 Armd Fld Arty Bn, Mar 1944		USA 3.44
667	6.43	USA only, disbanded June 1944, personnel to 125 Inf Bn		USA 6.44
668	6.43	USA only, redesignated 428 Armd Fld Arty Bn, Mar 1944		USA 3.44
669	6.43 T	USA only, disbanded Nov 1944		USA 11.44
670	6.43	Hawaii (1.45), disbanded Apr 1945		Hawaii 4.45
671	6.43	Hawaii (1.45), Philippines (7.45),	Philippine Islands	USA 1.46
672	6.43	USA only, redesignated 672 Amphibious Tractor Bn, Apr 1944		USA 4.44
679	6.43 T	N.Fr (1.45), It (3.45),	Bolzanetto, Italy	USA 10.45
691	12.41 LSP	UK (8.44), N.Fr (8.44),	Offenbach, Germany	USA 4.46
692	4.42 LSP	UK (9.44), N.Fr (9.44),	Brauweiler, Germany	USA 2.46
701	12.41 HSP	UK (6.42), N.Af (12.42), It (10.43), USA (8.45)	at sea	USA 10.45
702	12.41 HSP	UK (2.44), N.Fr (6.44),	Glehn, Germany	USA 10.45
703	12.41 HSP	UK (9.43), N.Fr (7.44),	Cologne, Germany	USA 1.46
704	12.41 HSP	UK (3.44), N.Fr (7.44),	Ulmen, Germany	USA 10.45
705	12.41 HSP	UK (5.44), N.Fr (7.44),	Trois Vierges, Lux'g	USA 11.45
706	3.42 HSP	USA only, disbanded, pers to 539,540,720 Amphib. Tractor Bns		USA 4.44
771	12.41 HSP	UK (11.43), N.Fr (9.44),	Viersen, Germany	USA 12.45
772	12.41 HSP	UK (10.44), N.Fr (12.44), USA (7.45)	Cp San Luis Obispo	USA 9.45
773	12.41 HSP	UK (2.44), N.Fr (8.44),	Berresheim, Germany	USA 10.45
774	12.41 HSP	UK (6.44), N.Fr (8.44),	Thionville, France	USA 10.45
775	12.41 HSP	USA only, redesignated 728 Amphibious Tractor Bn, Apr 1944		USA 4.44
776	12.41 HSP	N.Af (1.43), It (9.43), N.Fr (10.44),	Insviller, Germany	USA 11.45
795	12.41 HSP	USA only, disbanded Hampton Roads Port of Embarkation		USA 4.44
801	12.41 HSP	UK (3.44), N.Fr (6.44),	Steinheim, Germany	USA 11.45
802	12.41 HSP	UK (4.44), N.Fr (7.44),	Wadersloh, Germany	USA 12.45
803	12.41 HSP	UK (6.43), N.Fr (7.44),	Luxembourg, Lux'g	USA 12.45

HISTORICAL SUMMARY

		History	Locn 8.45	Inactivated
804	12.41 HSP	UK (8.42), N.Af (3.43), It (2.44), USA (7.45)	Cp Hood, Texas	USA 12.45
805	12.41 HSP	UK (8.42), N.Af (1.43), It (10.44), USA (7.45)	Cp Hood, Texas	USA 11.45
806	3.42 HSP	Eniwetok Atoll (9.45), Philippines (10.45)	at sea	USA 1.46
807	3.42 HSP	UK (8.44), N.Fr (9.44), USA (7.45)	Cp Cooke, Calif.	USA 9.45
808	3.42 HSP	UK (8.44), N.Fr (9.44), USA (8.45)	Cp Howze, Texas	USA 9.45
809	3.42	UK (12.44), N.Fr (1.45), USA (7.45)	Cp Bowie, Texas	USA 9.45
810	3.42	USA only, disbanded Dec 1943, personnel to other TD units		USA 12.43
811	4.42 HSP	N.Fr (9.44),	Beurig, Germany	USA 2.46
812	4.42 HSP	USA only, Towed guns 3.44, redes. 812 Tank Bn, Nov 1944		USA 11.44
813	12.41 HSP	UK (8.42), N.Af (12.42), Sic (7.43), UK (12.43), N.Fr (6.44) (POW Escort duty in Sicily, no guns or equipment)	Bocholtz, Germany	USA 11.45
814	5.42 HSP	UK (2.44), N.Fr (8.44),	Esch, Germany	Germany 9.45
815	5.42 HSP	Towed guns (1943?), New Guinea (3.44),		NGuin 9.44
816	5.42 HSP	Towed guns (3.44), USA only		USA 2.45
817	6.42 HSP	UK (7.44), N.Fr (8.44),	Warburg, Germany	USA 4.46
818	12.41 HSP	UK (11.43), N.Fr (7.44),	Burik, Germany	USA 10.45
819	6.42 HSP	Hawaii (3.44), Palau Islands (2.45),	Palau Islands	Palau 11.45
820	6.42 HSP	UK (10.44), N.Fr (10.44), USA (7.45)	Cp Swift, Texas	USA 9.45
821	6.42 HSP	UK (4.44), N.Fr (6.44),	Rheydt, Germany	USA 2.46
822	6.42 HSP	UK (12.44), N.Fr (1.45), USA (7.45)	Cp Gruber, Okla.	USA 9.45
823	7.42 HSP	UK (4.44), N.Fr (6.44),	Echt, Holland	USA 10.45
824	8.42 HSP	N.Fr (10.44), USA (7.45)	Ft Jackson, S.C.	USA 9.45
825	8.42 HSP	UK (6.44), N.Fr (7.44),	Verdun, France	USA 3.46
826	12.41 HSP	USA only, redesignated 826 Amphibious Tractor Bn, Apr 1944		USA 4.44
827	4.42 HSP	N.Fr (11.44),	Sarrebourg, France	USA 12.45
828	5.42 HSP	USA only, disb. with pers. to 150,373,390,393,394 QM Coys		USA 12.43
829	7.42 HSP	USA only, disb. with pers. to 8 Service Command		USA 3.44
846	12.41 HSP	USA only, disb. with pers. to VIII Corps, 3rd Army		USA 12.43
893	12.41 HSP	UK (1.44), N.Fr (7.44), (ex TD Center)	Altendorf, Germany	USA 2.46
894	12.41 HSP	UK (8.42), N.Af (1.43), It (9.43),	Piancenza, Italy	Italy 9.45
899	12.41 HSP	N.Af (1.43), UK (12.43), N.Fr (D-Day)	Venwegen, Germany	USA 12.45

Organisation on Formation :

  LT = Light Towed   LT* = Lt Towed to SP in 1942 when equipment available   SP = Self-Propelled

  T = Towed   HSP = Heavy Self-Propelled   LSP = Light Self-Propelled

TANK DESTROYER BATTALIONS - CAMPAIGN SUMMARY

NORTH AFRICA & EUROPE		601	602	603	605	607	609	610	612	614	628	629	630	631	633	634	635	636	638	643	644	645	648	654	656	661	679	691	692	701	702	703	704	705	771	772	773	774	776	801	802	803	804	805	807
Algeria-Fr.Morocco	11.42	*																												*															
Tunisia	11.42-5.43	*																												*											*			*	
Sicily	7.43-8.43	*																																											
Naples-Foggia	9.43-1.44	*																*				*								*											*			*	*
Anzio	1.44-5.44	*		*														*				*								*														*	*
Rome-Arno	1.44-9.44	*																*				*								*											*		*	*	*
Southern France	8.44-9.44	*																*																											
North Apennines	9.44-4.45																												*				*										*	*	
Po Valley	4.45-5.45																												*				*										*	*	
Normandy	6.44-7.44			*		*			*			*	*			*	*				*		*									*			*	*	*			*		*	*	*	
Northern France	7.44-9.44		*	*		*	*	*	*	*	*	*	*	*	*	*	*			*	*		*									*			*	*	*	*	*	*	*	*	*	*	
Rhineland	9.44-3.45	*	*	*	*	*	*	*	*	*	*	*	*	*	*	*	*	*	*	*	*	*	*	*	*	*		*		*	*	*	*	*	*	*	*	*	*	*	*	*	*	*	*
Ardennes-Alsace	12.44-1.45	*	*	*		*	*	*	*	*	*	*	*	*	*	*	*	*	*	*	*	*	*							*	*		*	*	*	*		*	*	*	*	*	*	*	*
Central Europe	3.45-5.45	*	*	*	*	*	*	*	*	*	*	*	*	*	*	*	*	*	*	*	*	*	*	*		*		*		*	*		*	*	*	*	*	*	*	*	*	*	*	*	*

NORTH AFRICA & EUROPE (contd)		808	809	811	813	814	817	818	820	821	822	823	824	825	827	893	894	899
Algeria-Fr.Morocco	11.42																	
Tunisia	11.42-5.43				*												*	*
Sicily	7.43-8.43																	
Naples-Foggia	9.43-1.44																*	
Anzio	1.44-5.44																	
Rome-Arno	1.44-9.44					*											*	*
Southern France	8.44-9.44																	
North Apennines	9.44-4.45																*	
Po Valley	4.45-5.45																*	
Normandy	6.44-7.44				*			*				*				*		*
Northern France	7.44-9.44				*	*	*	*		*		*		*		*		*
Rhineland	9.44-3.45	*	*	*	*	*	*	*	*	*	*	*	*	*	*	*		*
Ardennes-Alsace	12.44-1.45			*	*	*	*		*	*		*	*	*	*	*		*
Central Europe	3.45-5.45	*	*	*	*	*	*	*	*	*	*	*	*	*	*	*		*

PACIFIC THEATRE		632	637	640	641	671	815	819
Papua	7.42-1.43				*			
New Guinea	1.43-12.44	*			*			
Bismark Archpgo.	12.43-11.44			*	*			
Leyte	10.44-7.45	*						
Luzon	12.44-7.45	*	*					
S.Philippines	2.45-7.45		*	*		*	*	
Fiji	6.42	*						
Espiritu Santo	7.44	*						
Bourgainville	10.44	*						
Hawaii	3.44							*
Hawaii	1.45					*		
Palau Islands	2.45							*

M3 75mm GMC of 1st Marine Special Weapons Battalion, Cape Gloucester landings, New Britain, December 1943.
The camouflage scheme was unique to the Pacific.
Note additional .5cal AA machine guns.

M3 75mm GMC in typical Tunisian terrain. The 601st TD Bn was first into action in March 1943 at El Guettar. As more M10 vehicles were obtained, the M3's in many cases were passed to French units, short of anti-tank artillery at that time.

Hellcats stowed for travelling emplace on a reverse slope,
commanding the line of the opposite hills. Note slit trench
in foreground and setting of AA MG's, indicating the close
proximity of enemy forces.

An M18 on urban defence duty, France, September 1944. The AA
machine gun has been dismounted and fitted with an M3 tripod
for infantry role. The crewman covering the machine gunner
has an M3 sub-machine gun, not normally issued to SP units.

This M10, pictured at Mignano, Italy, is emplaced in a deep gun-pit, typical of those constructed when supporting Field Artillary for long periods, up to three months being known.

The M10 and M36 compared. Note the longer gun, heavier
mantlet and larger turret counterbalance on the M36 to
the rear of the M10.

The proposed 'Super Hellcat' with a 90mm M36 turret
Mounted on an M18 hull. Under evaluation in 1945, this
vehicle does not appear to have had combat trials.

An M36 90mm GMC at speed. Introduced into combat in October 1944
and intermixed with M10's until sufficient numbers were available
for units to completely convert. The 90mm gun was capable of
taking on enemy Panther and Tiger tanks.

TANK DESTROYER BATTALION - LIGHT - <u>PERSONNEL</u> - DECEMBER 1941

T/O 18-16 24th December 1941	Bn HQ	HEADQUARTERS & HQ COMPANY								REMARKS
		Coy HQ		Comms Pln	Staff Pln			Maint Pln	Transp Pln	Staff Pln Sections Administration Intelligence & Opns Supply
		HQ	Motor Maint		Adm	Int	Sup			
Lieutenant colonel	1	-	-	-	-	-	-	-	-	
Major	1	-	-	-	-	-	-	-	-	
Captain	3	1	-	-	-	-	-	-	-	
First lieutenant	-	1	-	1	-	-	-	1	-	
Second lieutenant	-	-	-	-	1	-	-	-	1	
:armed										
Pistol .45cal	5	2	-	1	1	-	-	1	1	
Warrant officer	-	-	-	-	-	-	-	-	-	
Master sergeant	-	-	-	-	1	-	-	1	-	
First sergeant	-	1	-	-	-	-	-	-	-	no rocket projectors
Technical sergeant	-	-	-	1	1	1	1	-	-	
Staff sergeant	-	1	1	-	-	-	-	1	1	
:armed										
Pistol .45cal	-	2	1	1	2	1	1	2	1	
Sergeant	-	1p	-	1p	-	-	2	2	-	
Corporal	-	2	-	1	-	1	1	-	3	
:armed										
Pistol .45cal	-	1	-	1	-	-	2	2	-	
Carbine .3cal (r)	-	1	-	1	-	1	1	-	3	(r) substitute rifle .3cal
Carbine .3cal (s)	-	1	-	-	-	-	-	-	-	(s) substitute sub MG .45cal
other ranks	-	27	4	17	11	16	6	17	35	
:armed										
Pistol .45cal	-	6	-	3	-	8	1	-	1	
Carbine .3cal (r)	-	12	2	8	8	4	2	10	1	
Carbine .3cal (s)	-	9	2	6	3	4	3	7	33	

TANK DESTROYER BATTALION - LIGHT - PERSONNEL - DECEMBER 1941

T/O 18-17 & 18-18 24th December 1941	TANK DESTROYER COMPANY (x3)				PIONEER COMPANY				ATTACHED MEDIC T/O 18-15
	Coy HQ		3x TD Plns (ea)		Coy HQ		Pioneer Pln (x3)		
	HQ Sec	Motor Maint	Pln HQ	2x Gun sects (ea)	HQ Sec	Motor Maint	Pln HQ	3x Pioneer sect (ea)	
Lieutenant colonel	-	-	-	-	-	-	-	-	-
Major	-	-	-	-	-	-	-	-	-
Captain	1	-	-	-	1	-	-	-	1
First lieutenant	1	-	-	-	1	-	-	-	1
Second lieutenant	-	-	1	-	-	-	1	-	-
:armed									
Pistol .45cal	2	-	1	-	2	-	1	-	
Warrant officer	-	-	-	-	-	-	-	-	-
Master sergeant	-	-	-	-	-	-	-	-	
First sergeant	1	-	-	-	1	-	-	-	
Technical sergeant	-	-	-	-	-	-	-	-	
Staff sergeant	1	1	1	-	1	1	1	-	1
:armed									
Pistol .45cal	2	1	1	-	2	1	1	-	
Sergeant	2	-	1	1	2	-	-	1	-
Corporal	2	-	4	1	2	-	-	1	1
:armed									
Pistol .45cal	2p	-	-	-	2p	-	-	-	
Carbine .3cal (r)	1	-	5	2	1	-	-		
Carbine .3cal (s)	1	-	-	-	1	-	-		
other ranks	19	4	17	8	19	4	10	10	20
:armed									
Pistol .45cal	2	-	3	6	1	-	1	-	
Carbine .3cal (r)	10	2	7	-	10	2	6	8	
Carbine .3cal (s)	7	2	7	2	8	2	3	2	

TANK DESTROYER BATTALION - HEAVY - <u>PERSONNEL</u> - DECEMBER 1941

T/O 18-26 24th December 1941	Bn HQ	HEADQUARTERS & HQ COMPANY								REMARKS

		Coy HQ		Comms
				Pln
					Staff Pln			Maint
								Pln
									Transp
									Pln
										Staff Pln Sections:
										    Administration
										    Intelligence & Opns
										    Supply

		HQ	Motor Maint		Adm	Int	Sup			
Lieutenant colonel	1	-	-	-	-	-	-	-	-	Attached Medic as Light Bn
Major	1	-	-	-	-	-	-	-	-	
Captain	4	1	-	-	-	-	-	-	-	
First lieutenant	-	1	-	-	-	-	-	1	-	
Second lieutenant	-	-	-	1	1	-	-	-	1	
:armed										
Pistol .45cal	6	2	-	1	1	-	-	1	1	
Warrant officer	-	-	-	-	-	-	-	-	-	
Master sergeant	-	-	-	-	1	-	-	1	-	
First sergeant	-	1	-	-	-	-	-	-	-	
Technical sergeant	-	-	-	1	1	1	1	-	-	
Staff sergeant	-	1	1	1	-	-	-	1	1	
:armed										
Pistol .45cal	-	2	1	2	2	1	1	2	1	no rocket projectors
Sergeant	-	1p	-	1p	-	1p	2	2	-	
Corporal	-	2	-	1	-	1	1r	-	3	
:armed										
Pistol .45cal	-	1	-	1	-	1	2	2	3	
Carbine .3cal (r)	-	1	-	1	-	1	1	-	-	(r) substitute rifle .3cal
Carbine .3cal (s)	-	1	-	-	-	-	-	-	-	(s) substitute sub MG .45cal
other ranks	-	29	4	17	10	15	6	18	32	
:armed										
Pistol .45cal	-	7	-	5	-	7	1	-	1	
Carbine .3cal (r)	-	13	2	3	7	4	2	13	3	
Carbine .3cal (s)	-	9	2	9	3	4	3	5	28	

TANK DESTROYER BATTALION - HEAVY - PERSONNEL - DECEMBER 1941

T/O 18-27 & 18-28 24th December 1941	TANK DESTROYER COMPANY (x3)								RECONNAISSANCE COY				
	Coy HQ		Lt TD Pln (x1)			Hy TD Pln (x2) ea			Coy HQ		Pioneer Pln		3x Recce Plns (ea)
	HQ	Motor Maint	Pln HQ	2x Gun sect (ea)	AA	Pln HQ	2x Gun sect (ea)	AA	HQ	Motor Maint	Pln HQ	2x Pioneer sect (tot)	
Lieutenant colonel	-	-	-	-	-	-	-	-	-	-	-	-	-
Major	-	-	-	-	-	-	-	-	1	-	-	-	-
Captain	1	-	-	-	-	-	-	-	1	-	-	-	-
First lieutenant	1	-	-	-	-	-	-	-	1	-	-	1	-
Second lieutenant	-	-	1	-	-	1	-	-	-	-	-	-	1
:armed													
Pistol .45cal	2	-	1	-	-	1	-	-	2	-	-	1	1
Warrant officer	-	-	-	-	-	-	-	-	-	-	-	-	-
Master sergeant	-	-	-	-	-	-	-	-	-	-	-	-	-
First sergeant	1	-	-	-	-	-	-	-	1	-	-	-	-
Technical sergeant	-	-	-	-	-	-	-	-	-	-	-	-	-
Staff sergeant	1	1	1	-	-	1	-	-	1	1	-	1	1
:armed													
Pistol .45cal	2	1	1	-	-	1	-	-	2	1	-	1	1
Sergeant	2p	-	1	1	1	1	1	1	2p	-	-	2p	2
Corporal	2	-	3	1	1	3	1	1	2	-	-	2	-
:armed													
Pistol .45cal	2	-	-	2	2	-	2	2	2	-	-	2	2
Carbine .3cal (r)	1	-	1	-	-	1	-	-	2	-	-	2	-
Carbine .3cal (s)	1	-	3	-	-	3	-	-	-	-	-	-	-
other ranks	22	4	15	6	6	15	6	6	23	3	-	22	21
:armed													
Pistol .45cal	1	-	1	4	4	1	4	4	4	-	-	1	6
Carbine .3cal (r)	12	2	9	-	-	9	-	-	12	2	-	16	7
Carbine .3cal (s)	9	2	5	2	2	5	2	2	7	1	-	5	8

TANK DESTROYER BATTALION - PERSONNEL - JUNE 1942

TO 18-26 : 8th June 1942	Bn HQ	HEADQUARTERS & HQ COMPANY								REMARKS

		Coy HQ		Comms Pln	Staff Pln			Maint Pln	Transp Pln	Staff platoon comprises :
										  Administration
										  Intelligence & Operations
										  Supply

		HQ	Motor Maint		Adm	Int	Sup			
Lieutenant colonel	1	-	-	-	-	-	-	-	-	
Major	1	-	-	-	-	-	-	-	-	
Captain	4	1	-	-	-	-	-	-	-	
First lieutenant	-	1	-	1	-	2	-	1	-	
Second lieutenant	-	-	-	-	1	-	-	-	1	
:armed Pistol .45cal	6	2	-	1	1	2	-	1	1	
Warrant officer	-	-	-	-	-	-	-	-	-	
Master sergeant	-	-	-	-	1	-	-	1p	-	sub-machine gun .45cal may be substituted for Carbine .3cal
First sergeant	-	1	-	-	-	-	-	-	-	
Technical sergeant	-	-	-	1	1	2	1	-	-	
Staff sergeant	-	1	1	1	-	-	-	1	1	
: armed Pistol .45cal	-	2	1	2	2	2	1	1	-	
Carbine .3cal	-	-	-	-	-	-	-	1	1	
Sergeant	-	1c	-	-	-	-	2	2	-	
Corporal	-	2	-	1	-	-	-	-	-	
: armed Carbine .3cal	-	2	-	1	-	-	2	2	-	
Rifle .3cal	-	1	-	-	-	-	-	-	-	
other ranks	-	22	7	14	7	18	6	20	36	
: armed Carbine .3cal	-	21	7	12	7	12	6	16	29	
Rifle .3cal	-	1	-	2	-	6	-	4	7	

TANK DESTROYER BATTALION - PERSONNEL - JUNE 1942

TO 18-27, 18-28
: 8th June 1942

	TANK DESTROYER COY (x3)								RECONNAISSANCE COY				
	Coy HQ		Lt TD Pln (x1)			Hy TD Pln x2 (ea)			Coy HQ		Pioneer Pln		3x Recce Plns (ea)
	HQ	Motor Maint	Pln HQ	2x Gun sect (ea)	AA	Pln HQ	2x Gun sect (ea)	AA	HQ	Motor Maint	Pln HQ	2x Pioneer sect (ea)	
Lieutenant colonel	-	-	-	-	-	-	-	-	-	-	-	-	-
Major	-	-	-	-	-	-	-	-	-	-	-	-	-
Captain	1	-	-	-	-	-	-	-	1	-	-	-	-
First lieutenant	1	-	1	-	-	-	-	-	1	-	1	-	1
Second lieutenant	-	-	-	-	-	1	-	-	-	-	-	-	-
: armed													
Pistol .45cal	2	-	1	-	-	1	-	-	2	-	1	-	1
Warrant officer	-	-	-	-	-	-	-	-	-	-	-	-	-
Master sergeant	-	-	-	-	-	-	-	-	-	-	-	-	-
First sergeant	1p	-	-	-	-	-	-	-	1	-	-	-	-
Technical sergeant	-	-	-	-	-	-	-	-	-	-	-	-	-
Staff sergeant	2	1	1	-	-	1	-	-	2	1	1	-	1
: armed													
Pistol .45cal	2	1	-	-	-	-	-	-	3	1	-	-	-
Carbine .3cal	1	-	1	-	-	1	-	-	-	-	1	-	1
Sergeant	2	-	1r	1	1	1r	1	1	1	-	-	1	2
Corporal	1c	-	3	1	1	3	1	1	2	-	-	1	-
: armed													
Carbine .3cal	1	-	1	2	2	1	2	2	3	-	-	2	2
Rifle .3cal	1	-	3	-	-	3	-	-	-	-	-	-	-
Pistol .45cal	1	-	-	-	-	-	-	-	-	-	-	-	-
other ranks	22	6	17	6	6	17	8	6	17	5	4	10	24
:armed													
Carbine .3cal	20	5	15	5	5	13	6	5	14	4	3	8	15
Rifle .3cal	2	1	2	1	1	4	2	1	3	1	1	2	9

TANK DESTROYER BATTALION (SP) - PERSONNEL - JANUARY 1943

TO 18-26 : 27th January 1943	Bn HQ	HEADQUARTERS & HQ COMPANY								REMARKS

		Coy HQ		Comms Pln	Staff Pln			Maint Pln	Transp Pln	Staff platoon sections :
										  Administration
										  Intelligence & operations
										  Supply

		HQ	Motor Maint		Adm	Int	Sup			
Lieutenant colonel	1	-	-	-	-	-	-	-	-	
Major	1	-	-	-	-	-	-	-	-	
Captain	4	1	-	-	-	-	-	-	-	
First lieutenant	-	1	-	1	-	2	-	1	-	
Second lieutenant	-	-	-	-	-	-	-	-	-	launcher, rocket, 2.36in
: armed										
Pistol .45cal	6	2	-	1	-	2	-	1	1	14 per HQ Coy
										9 per TD Coy
Warrant officer	-	-	-	-	1	-	-	-	-	21 per Recce Coy
Master sergeant	-	-	-	-	1	-	-	1	-	
First sergeant	-	1	-	-	-	-	-	-	-	for other armament refer
Technical sergeant	-	-	-	1	1	2	1	-	-	to 'vehicles' section
Staff sergeant	-	2	1	-	-	-	1	1	1	
: armed										
Pistol .45cal	-	3	1	1	3	2	2	2	1	
Sergeant	-	-	-	1	-	-	1	2	1	
Corporal	-	1	-	1	-	-	-	-	-	
: armed										
Carbine .3cal	-	1	-	2	-	-	1	2	1	
other ranks	-	19	4	9	2	13	5	17	23	
: armed										
Carbine .3cal	-	19	4	9	2	13	5	17	23	

TANK DESTROYER BATTALION (SP) - PERSONNEL - JANUARY 1943

TO 18-27, 18-28
: 27th January 1943

	TANK DESTROYER COY (x3)				RECONNAISSANCE COY				
	Coy HQ		3x TD Plns (ea)		Coy HQ		Pioneer Pln		3x Recce Plns (ea)
	HQ Sec	Motor Maint	Pln HQ	2x Gun sects (ea)	HQ Sec	Motor Maint	Pln HQ	2x Pioneer sects (ea)	
Lieutenant colonel	-	-	-	-	-	-	-	-	-
Major	-	-	-	-	-	-	-	-	-
Captain	1	-	-	-	1	-	-	-	-
First lieutenant	-	-	1	-	1	-	1	-	-
Second lieutenant	1	-	-	-	-	-	-	-	1
: armed									
Pistol .45cal	2	-	1	-	2	-	1	-	1
Warrant officer	-	-	-	-	-	-	-	-	-
Master sergeant	-	-	-	-	-	-	-	-	-
First sergeant	1	-	-	-	1	-	-	-	-
Technical sergeant	-	-	-	-	-	-	-	-	-
Staff sergeant	3	1	1	-	3	1	1	-	1
: armed									
Pistol .45cal	4	1	1	-	4	1	-	-	-
Carbine .3cal	-	-	-	-	-	-	1	-	1
Sergeant	1	-	1	2	-	-	-	1	2
Corporal	1	-	1	2	2	-	-	-	-
: armed									
Carbine .3cal	2	-	2	4	2	-	-	1	2
other ranks	23	6	8	6	22	4	3	10	14
: armed									
Carbine .3cal	23	6	4	6	22	4	3	10	12
Rifle .3cal	-	-	4	-	-	-	-	-	2

TANK DESTROYER BATTALION (SP) - PERSONNEL - MARCH 1944

TO & E 18-26 : 15th March 1944	Bn HQ	HEADQUARTERS & HQ COY							
		Coy HQ		Comms Pln	Staff Pln			Maint Pln	Transp Pln
		HQ	Motor Maint		Adm	Int	Sup		
Lieutenant colonel	1	-	-	-	-	-	-	-	-
Major	2	-	-	-	-	-	-	-	-
Captain	2	1	-	-	-	-	-	1	-
First lieutenant	1	1	-	1	-	2	-	-	-
Second lieutenant	-	-	-	-	-	-	-	-	1
: armed									
Pistol .45cal	6	2	-	1	-	2	-	1	1
Warrant officer	-	-	-	-	1	-	-	1	-
Master sergeant	-	-	-	-	1	-	-	1	-
First sergeant	-	1	-	-	-	-	-	-	-
Technical sergeant	-	-	-	1	1	2	1	1	-
Staff sergeant	2	-	1	1	-	-	1	-	-
: armed									
Pistol .45cal	2	1	1	2	3	2	2	3	-
Sergeant	-	-	-	1	-	-	1	-	1
Corporal	-	1	-	1	-	-	-	-	1
: armed									
Carbine .3cal	-	1	-	2	-	-	1	-	2
other ranks	-	16	4	7	2	9	7	3	39
: armed									
Carbine .3cal	-	6	1	4	-	7	5	1	-
Rifle .3cal	-	10	3	3	2	2	2	2	39

REMARKS

Staff platoon sections :
  Administration
  Intelligence & operations
  Supply

launcher, rocket, 2.36in

  14 per HQ Coy
  9 per TD Coy
  21 per Recce Coy

for other armament refer to 'vehicles' section

TANK DESTROYER BATTALION (SP) - _PERSONNEL_ - MARCH 1944

TO & E 18-27, 18-28 : 15th March 1944	TANK DESTROYER COY (x3)				RECONNAISSANCE COY				
	Coy HQ		3x TD Plns (ea)		Coy HQ		Pioneer Pln		3x Recce Plns (ea)
	HQ Sec	Motor Maint	Pln HQ	2x Gun sects (ea)	HQ Sec	Motor Maint	Pln HQ	2x Pioneer sects (ea)	
Lieutenant Colonel	-	-	-	-	-	-	-	-	-
Major	-	-	-	-	-	-	-	-	-
Captain	1	-	-	-	1	-	-	-	-
First lieutenant	-	-	1	-	1	-	-	-	-
Second lieutenant	1	-	-	-	-	-	1	-	1
: armed									
Pistol .45cal	2	-	1	-	2	-	1	-	1
Warrant officer	-	-	-	-	-	-	-	-	-
Master sergeant	-	-	-	-	-	-	-	-	-
First sergeant	1	-	-	-	1	-	-	-	-
Technical sergeant	-	1	-	-	-	-	-	-	-
Staff sergeant	3	1	1	-	3	-	1	-	1
: armed									
Pistol .45cal	4	2	1	-	4	-	1	-	1
Sergeant	1	-	1	2r	-	-	-	1	2
Corporal	1	-	1	2	2	-	-	1	-
: armed									
Carbine .3cal	2	-	-	2	2	-	-	2	-
Rifle .3cal	-	-	-	2	-	-	-	-	2
other ranks	22	7	7	4	25	4	3	6	19
: armed									
Carbine .3cal	8	2	1	4	11	1	1	5	11
Rifle .3cal	14	5	6	-	14	3	2	1	8

TANK DESTROYER BATTALION (TOWED) - <u>PERSONNEL</u> - <u>MAY 1943</u>

TO 18-36 : 7th May 1943	Bn HQ	HEADQUARTERS & HQ COY								REMARKS

		Coy HQ	2x Recce Plns (ea)	Comms Pln	Staff Pln			Maint Pln	Transp Pln	Staff platoon sections :
										    Administration
										    Intelligence & Operations
										    Supply

					Adm	Int	Sup			
Lieutenant colonel	1p	-	-	-	-	-	-	-	-	
Major	2p	-	-	-	-	-	-	-	-	
Captain	2	1	-	-	-	-	-	-	-	
First lieutenant	2	1	1	1	-	2	-	-	-	
Second lieutenant	-	-	-	-	-	-	-	-	1	
: armed										launcher, rocket, 2.36in
Pistol .45cal	3	-	-	-	-	-	-	-	-	26 per HQ Coy
Sub MG .45cal	4	2	1	1	-	2	-	-	1	15 per TD Coy
Warrant officer	-	-	-	-	1	-	-	1	-	for other armament refer
Master sergeant	-	-	-	-	1	-	-	1	-	to 'vehicles' section
First sergeant	-	1	-	-	-	-	-	-	-	
Technical sergeant	-	-	-	1	1	2	1	-	-	
Staff sergeant	-	2	1	-	-	-	1	2	1	
: armed										
Sub MG .45cal	-	3	1	1	3	2	2	4	1	
Sergeant	-	-	2	1	-	-	1	2	1	
Corporal	-	1	-	1	-	-	-	-	-	
: armed										
Sub MG .45cal	-	1	2	2	-	-	1	2	1	
other ranks	-	27	18	9	2	13	5	17	19	
: armed										
Rifle .3cal	-	14	2	-	-	-	-	-	-	
Sub MG .45cal	-	13	16	9	2	13	5	17	19	

TANK DESTROYER BATTALION (TOWED) - PERSONNEL - MAY 1943   NOTES ON PERSONAL WEAPONS

TO 18-37 : 7th May 1943	TANK DESTROYER COY (x3)			
	Coy HQ		3x TD Plns (ea)	
	HQ Sec	Motor Maint	Pln HQ	2x Gun sects (ea)
Lieutenant colonel	-	-	-	-
Major	-	-	-	-
Captain	1	-	-	-
First lieutenant	-	-	1	-
Second lieutenant	1	-	-	-
: armed				
Sub MG .45cal	2	-	1	-
Warrant officer	-	-	-	-
Master sergeant	-	-	-	-
First sergeant	1	-	-	-
Technical sergeant	-	-	-	-
Staff sergeant	3	1	1	-
: armed				
Sub MG .45cal	4	1	1	-
Sergeant	1	-	1r	2
Corporal	2	-	1	2
: armed				
Sub MG .45cal	3	-	2	-
Rifle .3cal	-	-	1	-
Carbine .3cal	-	-	-	4
other ranks	31	5	8	16
: armed				
Sub MG .45cal	13	5	4	-
Rifle .3cal	18	-	4	-
Carbine .3cal	-	-	-	16

NOTES ON PERSONAL WEAPONS

Rifle, .3cal, M1903

   Bolt operated rifle of WW1 vintage.
   Magazine of 5 rounds. Also used with
   grenade launcher M1.

Rifle, .3cal, M1 (Garand)

   Replacement for the M1903 above.
   Semi-automatic, gas operated,
   8 rounds per magazine, approx rate
   of fire 20 rounds per minute. The
   effective range was about 500yds
   Used with grenade launcher M7

Carbine, .3cal, M1, (Winchester)

   Self loading weapon with magazine
   of 15 or 30 rounds and rate of fire
   of approx 30 rounds per minute.
   Used mainly in SP Tank Destroyer
   Bns and replaced to a large degree
   by the M1 rifle in later TO & E

Pistol, Automatic, .45cal, M1911A1

   Magazine fed (7 rounds), recoil
   operating, self-loading. Used by
   officers & senior NCO's, mainly
   in SP Tank Destroyer Bns

Sub-machine gun, .45cal, M3

   Vertically fed from 30 round
   magazine, max range approx 100yds,
   automatic fire only 350-540 rounds
   per minute. Used extensively in
   Towed Tank Destroyer Bns

TANK DESTROYER BATTALION (TOWED) - <u>PERSONNEL</u> - SEPTEMBER 1944

TO & E 18-36 : 1st September 1944	Bn HQ	HEADQUARTERS & HQ COY								REMARKS
		Coy HQ	2x Recce Plns (ea)	Comms Pln	Staff Pln			Maint Pln	Transp Pln	Staff platoon sections :
					Adm	Int	Sup			Administration
Lieutenant colonel	1p	-	-	-	-	-	-	-	-	Intelligence & Operations
Major	2p	-	-	-	-	-	-	-	-	Supply
Captain	2	1	-	-	-	-	-	1	-	
First lieutenant	2	-	1	1	-	2	-	-	-	
Second lieutenant	-	-	-	-	-	-	-	-	1	
: armed										launcher, rocket, 2.36in
Pistol .45cal	3	-	-	-	-	-	-	-	-	26 per HQ Coy
Sub MG .45cal	4	1	1	1	-	2	-	1	1	15 per TD Coy
Warrant officer	-	-	-	-	1	-	-	1	-	for other armament refer
Master sergeant	-	-	-	-	1	-	-	1	-	to 'vehicles' section
First sergeant	-	1	-	-	-	-	-	-	-	
Technical sergeant	-	1	-	1	1	2	1	1	-	
Staff sergeant	-	2	1	1	-	-	1	-	-	
: armed										
Sub MG .45cal	-	5	2	3	3	4	2	4	-	
Sargeant	-	-	2	1	-	-	1	-	1	
Corporal	-	1	-	1	-	-	-	-	1	
: armed										
Sub MG .45cal	-	1	2	2	-	-	1	-	2	
other ranks	-	19	18	8	2	16	6	17	18	
: armed										
Rifle .3cal	-	7	·2	-	-	-	-	-	-	
Sub MG .5cal	-	12	16	8	2	16	6	17	18	

37

TO & E 18-37 : 1st September 1944	TANK DESTROYER COY (x3)			
	Coy HQ		3x TD Plns (ea)	
	HQ Sec	Motor Maint	Pln HQ	2x Gun sects (ea)
Lieutenant colonel	-	-	-	-
Major	-	-	-	-
Captain	1	-	-	-
First lieutenant	-	-	1	-
Second lieutenant	1	-	-	-
: armed				
Sub MG .45cal	2	-	1	-
Warrant officer	-	-	-	-
Master sergeant	-	-	-	-
First sergeant	1	-	-	-
Technical sergeant	-	1	-	-
Staff sergeant	3	-	1	-
: armed				
Sub MG .45cal	4	1	1	-
Sergeant	1	-	1r	2
Corporal	2	-	1	2
: armed				
Rifle .3cal	-	-	1	-
Sub MG .45cal	3	-	1	-
Carbine .3cal	-	-	-	4
other ranks	21	6	8	16
: armed				
Rifle .3cal	9	-	4	-
Sub MG .45cal	12	6	4	-
Carbine .3cal	-	-	-	16

Lt. col.	one silver oak leaf
Major	one gold oak leaf
Captain	two silver bars
1st lieut.	one silver bar
2nd lieut.	one gold bar

NCO's insignia 80mm wide in light khaki or yellow silk on a blue patch

1st Sgt Master Sgt Tech. Sgt

Staff Sgt Technician 3 Sgt

Technician 4 Cpl. Technician 5

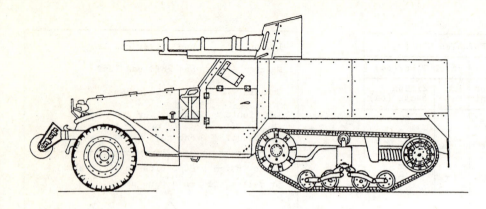

M3 75mm GMC

M18 GMC Hellcat

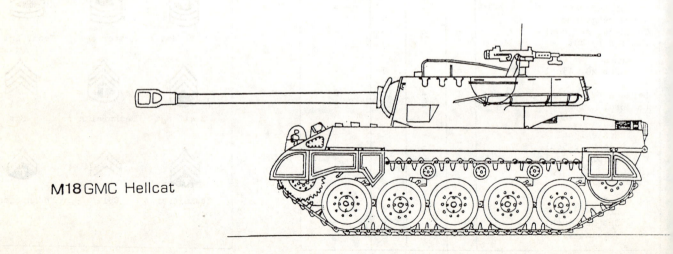

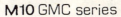
M10 GMC series

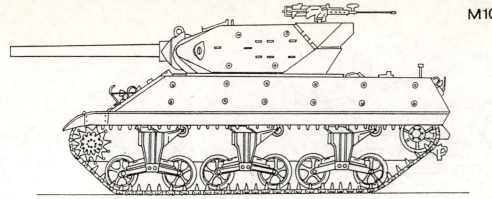

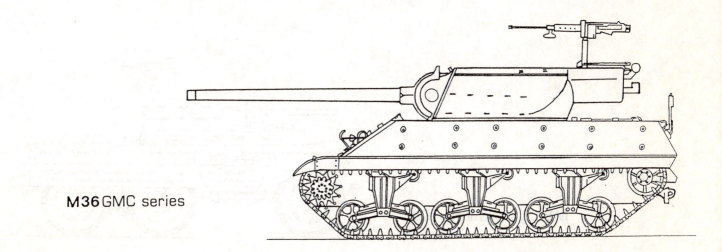

M36 GMC series

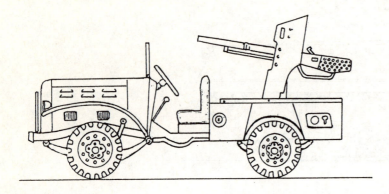

Dodge **M6** **37**mm GMC

M8 Light Armored Car

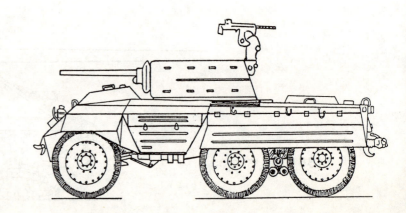

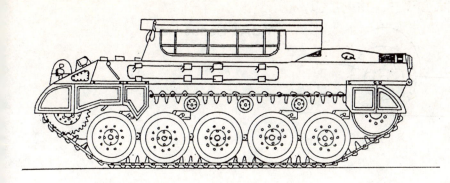

M39 Armored Utility

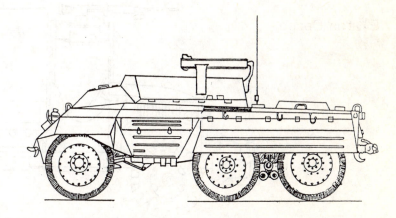

M20 Armored Utility

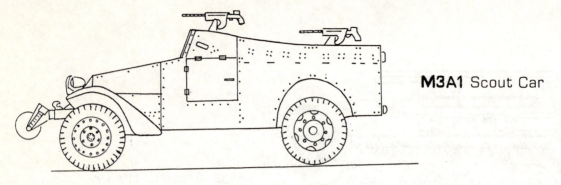

M3A1 Scout Car

2½ ton Cargo

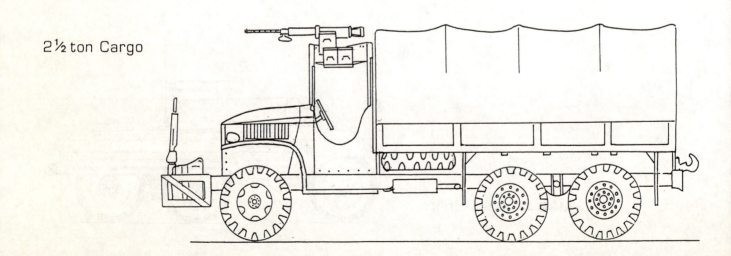

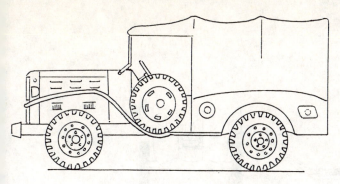

$\frac{3}{4}$ ton Weapons Carrier

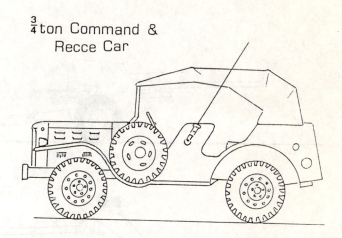

$\frac{3}{4}$ ton Command &
Recce Car

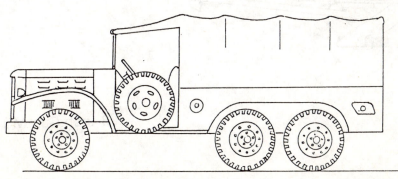

$1\frac{1}{2}$ ton Cargo

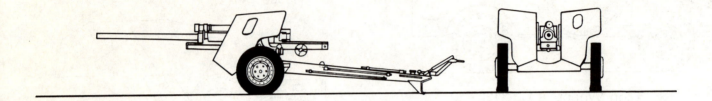

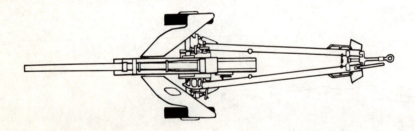

3-inch Gun M5

TD BATTALIONS - COMBAT EQUIPMENT - MAIN ORDNANCE TYPE

Bn No	M3	M10	M18	M36	3-inch	Remarks
601	*	*		*		
602			*			
603			*			
605				*	* 3.44	SP 3.45
607				*	* 12.43	SP 11.44
609			*			
610				*	* 12.43	SP 10.44
612			*		* 12.43	SP 12.44
614					*	
628		*		*		
629		*				
630		*		*		
631		*				
632		*				
633			*			
634		*				
635		*				
636		*		*		
637			*			
638			*			
640		*				
643			*		* 12.43	SP 12.44
644		*				
645		*		*		
648				*	* 3.44	SP 5.45
654		*		*		
656			*	*		
661			*			
671			*			SP 6.43
679					*	
691				*	* 12.43	SP 3.45
692		*			* 3.44	SP 3.45
701	*	*				
702		*		*		
703		*		*		
704			*			
705			*			
771		*		*		
772				*	*	SP 3.45
773		*		*		
774				*	* 12.43	SP 1.45
776	*	*		*		
801			*		* 12.43	SP 4.45
802				*	* 12.43	SP 3.45
803		*		*		
804		*				
805					* 9.44	(also M3)
806		*				
807					*	
808				*	* 7.43	SP 1.45
809			*	*		
811			*			
813	*	*		*		
814		*		*		
815					*	
817			*		* 7.43	SP 3.45
818		*		*		
819		*			* 7.43	SP 11.44
820			*		* 7.43	SP 3.45
821		*			* 7.43	SP 12.44
822			*		* 7.43	SP 4.45
823		*			* 7.43	SP 12.44
824			*		* 7.43	SP 3.45
825		*			* 7.43	SP 2.45
827			*		* 6.43	SP 7.44
893		*				
894	*	*				
899		*		*		

DESIGN & DEVELOPMENT SUMMARY - SP TANK DESTROYERS

PARENT	HULL	GUN	DESIGNATION	DIRIVITIES	DISPOSITION
Cleveland Hi-Speed Tractor	as parent	3 inch	T1 (M5) GMC	none	did not enter service
Dodge ¼-ton Truck	as parent	37mm	M6 (37mm) GMC	M2 (37mm) GMC - field conversion of M2 half-track by fitting the 37mm guns from the M6	reverted to trucks by removal of gun, approx 100 remained as Recce vehicles until replaced by M8 Armoured Cars
M3 Half Track	as parent	75mm M1897A or M1	T12 (M3) 75mm GMC	M3A1 GMC used M2A2 carriages instead of M3A3 carriages	replaced by M10, used by Hvy Tps of British Armd Car units, Italy and Free French units.
				T30 (75mm howz) HMC T19 (105mm howz) HMC	replaced by M8 HMC replaced by M7 HMC
		57mm M1	T48 57mm GMC SU-57 (USSR)		lease lend only
New Design	New Design	57mm M1	T49 57mm GMC	development vehicles only	cancelled in favour of T67 GMC
		75mm M3	T67 75mm GMC	development vehicles only	cancelled in favour of T70 GMC
		76mm M1	T70 (M18) 76mm GMC 'Hellcat'		served Italy, Pacific & NW Europe
		Gun & turret removed		T41 (M39) Armd Utility Vehicle	served with US Army post-war, incl Korea

NOTE :   GMC = Gun Motor Carriage   HMC = Howitzer Motor Carriage

SP TANK DESTROYER & ASSOCIATED VEHICLES - DESIGN & DEVELOPMENT

PARENT	HULL	GUN	DESIGNATION	DIRIVITIVES	DISPOSITION
M4A2 Medium Tank	thinner armour, angled sides	3 inch M7 gun in open topped turret	T35 (M10) GMC (Wolverine - UK)		In service N.Africa, Italy, NW.Europe & Pacific
		90mm M3	M36.B2 90mm GMC	(as M10 with new turret & gun)	In service May 1945
		17pdr	Achilles Mk IC	(as M10 with British 17pdr gun)	British service
M4A3 Medium Tank	thinner armour, angled sides	3 inch M7 gun in open topped turret	M10.A1 GMC		Retained in USA for training or converted to M35 Prime Mover
		90mm M3	M36 90mm GMC	(as M10.A1 with new turret & gun)	in service Nov 1944
		17 pdr	Achilles Mk IIC	(as M10.A1 with British 17pdr gun)	British service
		none	M35 Prime Mover (155mm, 240mm artillery)	(as M10.A1, no gun or turret)	Italy & NW.Europe, replaced by M6 38ton High Speed Tractor
	M4A3	90mm M3	M36.B1 90mm GMC	(as M4A3 with M36 turret & gun)	NW Europe

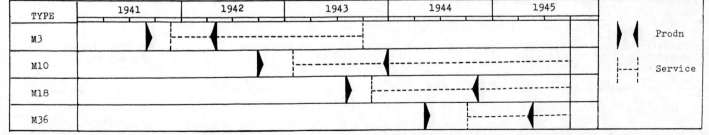

VEHICLE DATA

	M6 Dodge 4x4 37mm GMC	M3 75mm GMC	M18 76mm GMC Hellcat
WEIGHT	3.3 tons approx	8.9 tons approx	17.9 tons approx
ARMOUR	6mm gunshield only	6-13mm	7-25mm
ARMAMENT	1 x 37mm gun (80 rounds) Traverse 360 degrees Elevation +15/-10 degrees no secondary armament	1 x 75mm gun (59 rounds) Traverse L 21/R 23 degrees Elevation +25 degrees no secondary armament	1 x 76.2mm gun (45 rounds) Traverse 360 degrees Elevation +19½/-10 degrees 1 x .5cal MG (800 rounds)
ENGINE	Dodge T214 6cyl petrol (94hp)	White 160AX 6cyl petrol (147hp)	Continental R975.C4 petrol (400hp)
CREW	Commdr, driver, 2 x gunners	Commdr, driver, 3 x gunners	Commdr, driver, 3 x gunners
PRODUCTION	5380 (2.42-6.43), reverted to Dodge 4x4 trucks	2202 (6.41-5.43), many reverted to M3 half tracks	2507 (7.43-10.44)
SPEED RANGE	55 mph max 240 miles	45 mph max 200 miles	55 mph max 150 miles
LENGTH WIDTH HEIGHT	14ft 10ins 6ft 4ins 6ft 10ins	20ft 6ins 7ft 1in 8ft 2ins	17ft 10ins 9ft 5ins 8ft 5ins
VERT. STEP FORDING TRENCH GRADIENT	details as for Dodge 4x4	1ft 0in 2ft 8ins not applicable 60%	3ft 0in 4ft 0in 6ft 2ins 60%

PENETRATION OF
  PROJECTILE
	50mm (AP) at 30 degrees at
	500 yards
		70mm (AP) at 30 degrees at
		500 yards
			88mm (AP), 133mm (HVAP)
			  at 30 degrees at
			  1000 yards

VEHICLE DATA

	M10 & M10A1 GMC	M36 & M36B2 GMC	M36B1 GMC
WEIGHT	29.5 tons approx	27.7 tons approx	not known
ARMOUR	12-37mm	12-37mm	12mm min (turret), M4A3 hull
ARMAMENT	1 x 3in. M7 gun (54 rounds) Traverse 360 degrees, Elevation +19/-10 degrees	1 x 90mm M3 gun (47 rounds) Traverse 360 degrees, Elevation +20/-10 degrees	1 x 90mm M3 gun (47 rounds) Traverse 360 degrees, Elevation +20/-10 degrees
	1 x .5cal MG (300 rounds)	1 x .5cal MG (1000 rounds)	1 x .5cal MG (1000 rounds)
ENGINE	M10 : Twin GM6-71 12cyl diesels (375hp) M10A1 : Ford GAA V8 petrol (500hp)	M36 : Ford GAA V8 petrol (500hp) M36B2 : Twin GM6-71 12 cyl diesels (375hp)	M36B1 : Ford GAA V8 petrol (500hp)
CREW	Commdr, driver, 3 x gunners	Commdr, driver, 3 x gunners	Commdr, driver, 3 x gunners
PRODUCTION	M10 4993 (9.42-10.43) M10A1 1413 (10.42-11.43)	M36 1298 (4.44-6.45) M36B2 237 (4.44-5.44)	M36B1 187 (10.44-12.44)
SPEED RANGE	32 mph max 200 miles	30 mph max 150 miles	30 mph max 150 miles
LENGTH WIDTH HEIGHT	19ft 7ins 10ft 0in 8ft 2ins	20ft 2ins 10ft 0in 8ft 2ins	20ft 2ins 10ft 0in 8ft 2ins
VERT. STEP FORDING TRENCH GRADIENT	2ft 0in 3ft 0in 7ft 6ins 60%	2ft 0in 3ft 0in 7ft 6ins 60%	2ft 0in 3ft 0in 7ft 6ins 60%
PENETRATION OF PROJECTILE	102mm (APC) at 30 degrees at 1000 yards	120mm (APC), 195mm (HVAP) at 30 degrees at 1000 yards	120mm (APC), 195mm (HVAP) at 30 degrees at 1000 yards

TANK DESTROYER BATTALION - LIGHT - VEHICLES - DECEMBER 1941

T/O 18-16 24th December 1941	HEADQUARTERS & HQ COMPANY								REMARKS
	Coy HQ		Comms Pln	Staff Pln			Maint Pln	Trans Pln	
	HQ	Motor Maint		Adm	Int	Sup			
Gun, 37mm, ATk (towed)	-	-	-	-	-	-	-	-	Subs veh: Gun, 37mm, (SP)
Car, Armored, Command	-	-	-	-	2*^{4}	-	-	-	Subs veh; Car, scout
Motorcycle, solo	6	-	-	-	-	-	-	4	
Truck, Hvy Wrecker, 4ton	-	-	-	-	-	-	1	-	
Trucks:									
¼ton 4x4 (jeep)	1*	1	2*	-	-	-	2*	4*	
¼ton Command	2*1	-	3*1	2	2*1	1	1*	1	Subs veh: truck, ½ton
¼ton Weapons Carrier	1**	-	1**	1**	-	2**	-	-	Subs veh: truck, ½ton
Motor Air Compressor	-	-	-	-	-	-	-	-	
2½ton Cargo:									
Ammunition	-	-	-	-	-	-	-	3**	
Combat	-	-	-	-	-	-	-	5**	
Gasoline & oil	-	-	-	-	-	-	-	3*	
Kitchen	-	-	-	-	-	-	-	5*	* with .3cal MG
Maintenance	-	1**	-	-	-	-	2**	-	** with .5cal MG
Mines	-	-	-	-	-	-	-	2**	
Rations	-	-	-	-	-	-	-	1*	
Trailers:									
1ton, 2whl, cargo	-	-	-	-	-	-	-	14	

T/O 18-17 & 18-18 24th December 1941	TANK DESTROYER COMPANY (x3)				PIONEER COMPANY				ATTACHED MEDIC T/O 18-15
	Coy HQ		3x TD Plns (ea)		Coy HQ		Pioneer Pln (x3)		
	HQ	Motor Maint	Pln HQ	2x Gun sects (ea)	HQ	Motor Maint	Pln HQ	3x Pioneer sects (ea)	
Gun, 37mm, ATk, towed	-	-	-	2(nb)	-	-	-	-	-
Car, Armored, Command	-	-	-	-	-	-	-	-	-
Motorcycle, solo	4	-	-	-	4	-	-	-	-
Truck, Hvy Wrecker, 4ton	-	-	-	-	-	-	-	-	-
Truck:									
¼ton 4x4 (jeep)	1*	1	2*	-	1*	1*	1*	-	-
¾ton Command	2(1*)	-	1	-	2(1*)	-	1*	-	1
¾ton Weapons Carrier	1**	-	4(2*)	2(nb)	1**	-	1**	2**	-
Motor Air Compressor	-	-	-	-	1	-	-	-	1
2½ton Cargo:									
Ammunition	-	-	-	-	-	-	-	-	-
Combat	-	-	-	-	-	-	-	-	-
Gasoline & oil	-	-	-	-	-	-	-	-	-
Kitchen	-	-	-	-	-	-	-	-	-
Maintenance	-	1**	-	-	-	1**	-	-	-
Mines	-	-	-	-	-	-	-	-	-
Rations	-	-	-	-	-	-	-	-	-
Trailers:									
1ton, 2whl, cargo	-	-	1	-	1	-	1	1	-
Ambulance, cross country	-	-	-	-	-	-	-	-	1

(nb) each 37mm SP gun replaced 1x 37mm towed
    gun and 1x ¾ton Weapons Carrier

TANK DESTROYER BATTALION - HEAVY - VEHICLES - DECEMBER 1941

T/O 18-26 24th December 1941	HEADQUARTERS & HQ COMPANY								REMARKS
	Coy HQ		Comms Pln	Staff Pln			Maint Pln	Trans Pln	
	HQ	Motor Maint		Adm	Int	Sup			
Gun, 37mm, ATk, SP	-	-	-	-	-	-	-	-	Subs veh: 37mm GMC T-21 (nb)
Gun, 3-in, ATk, SP (M5)	-	-	-	-	-	-	-	-	Subs veh: 75mm GMC T-12
Gun, 37mm, AA, SP	-	-	-	-	-	-	-	-	Subs veh: M3 Carrier Pers, AA mount
Car, Armored, Command	1*	-	2*	-	4*	1*	-	-	Subs veh: Scout Car/Halftrack
Car, Armored, Personnel	-	-	1*	-	-	-	-	-	Subs veh: Halftrack Pers Carrier
Car, Armored, Recce, 37mm	-	-	-	-	-	-	-	-	Subs veh: Scout Car/ Halftrack
Truck, Hvy Wrecker, 4tons	-	-	-	-	-	-	2	-	
Trucks:									
¼ton 4x4 (jeep)	1*	1	-	-	-	-	2	3	
½ton Command	1	-	1	3	-	-	1	3	Subs veh: Truck - ½ton
¾ton Weapons Carrier	2**	-	-	-	-	2**	-	-	Subs veh: Truck - ½ton
2½ton Cargo:									
Ammunition	-	-	-	-	-	-	-	3**	
Combat	-	-	-	-	-	-	-	6**	
Gasoline & oil	-	-	-	-	-	-	-	3*	
Kitchen	-	-	-	-	-	-	-	5*	
Maintenance	-	1**	-	-	-	-	2**	-	
Radio Repair	-	-	1**	-	-	-	-	-	
Rations	-	-	-	-	-	-	-	1*	
Trailers:									
1ton, 2whl, cargo	-	-	-	-	-	-	-	12	1x ration, 3x Gas, 3x ammo, 5x Kitchen
Motorcycle, solo	5	-	4	-	-	-	-	4	

```
* with .3cal MG
** with .5cal MG
```

nb: T21 prototypes employing 37mm gun on ¼ton jeep with twin rear axles

TANK DESTROYER BATTALION - HEAVY - VEHICLES - DECEMBER 1941

T/O 18-27 & 18-28 24th December 1941	TANK DESTROYER COMPANY (x3)								RECONNAISSANCE COY				
	Coy HQ		Lt TD Pln (x1)			Hy TD Pln (x2) ea			Coy HQ		Pioneer Pln		3x Recce Plns (ea)
	HQ	Motor Maint	Pln HQ	2x Gun sect (ea)	AA	Pln HQ	2x Gun sect (ea)	AA	HQ	Motor Maint	Pln HQ	2x Pioneer sect (tot)	
Gun, 37mm, ATk, SP	-	-	-	2*	-	-	-	-	-	-	-	-	-
Gun, 3-in, ATk, SP (M5)	-	-	-	-	-	-	2*	-	-	-	-	-	-
Gun, 37mm, AA, SP	-	-	-	-	2	-	-	2	-	-	-	-	-
Car, Armored, Command	2*	-	2*	-	-	2*	-	-	2*	-	-	1	-
Car, Armored, Personnel	-	-	3*	-	-	3*	-	-	-	-	-	2*	-
Car, Armored, Recce, 37mm	-	-	-	-	-	-	-	-	-	-	-	-	2*
Truck, Hvy Wrecker, 4tons	-	-	-	-	-	-	-	-	-	-	-	-	-
Trucks:													
¼ton 4x4 (jeep)	1	1	-	-	-	-	-	-	1*	-	-	-	4**
¼ton Command	1	-	-	-	-	-	-	-	1*	-	-	-	-
¼ton Weapons Carrier	1*	-	-	-	-	-	-	-	-	-	-	2	-
2½ton Cargo:	1**	-	-	-	-	-	-	-	-	-	-	-	-
Ammunition	-	-	-	-	-	-	-	-	-	-	-	-	-
Combat	-	-	-	-	-	-	-	-	-	-	-	-	-
Gasoline & oil	-	-	-	-	-	-	-	-	-	-	-	-	-
Kitchen	-	-	-	-	-	-	-	-	-	-	-	-	-
Maintenance	-	1	-	-	-	-	-	-	-	1**	-	-	-
Radio repair	-	-	-	-	-	-	-	-	-	-	-	-	-
Rations	-	-	-	-	-	-	-	-	-	-	-	-	-
Trailers:													
1ton, 2whl, cargo	-	-	-	-	-	-	-	-	-	-	-	2	-
Motorcycle, solo	5	-	-	-	-	-	-	-	3	-	-	-	2

TANK DESTROYER BATTALION - VEHICLES - JUNE 1942

TO 18-26 : 8th June 1942	HEADQUARTERS & HQ COMPANY								REMARKS
	Coy HQ		Comms Pln	Staff Pln			Maint Pln	Transp Pln	see also page 10
	HQ	Motor Maint		Adm	Int	Sup			
Carriage, SP, 37mm (M6)	-	-	-	-	-	-	-	-	Subs veh 57mm Gun SP or 37mm gun towed by ¼ton wpns carrier
Carriage, SP, 3-in (M5)	-	-	-	-	-	-	-	-	Subs veh 75mm Gun SP, 37mm/57mm Gun SP or towed 37mm gun
GMC T1E4 (M13) .5cal AA MG	-	-	-	-	-	-	-	-	Subs veh ¼ton wpns carrier with twin .5cal AA MG
Car, Armored, Light, M3A1	-	-	-	1**	4**	-	-	-	Subs veh Car, half-track (M2)
Motorcycle - solo	2	-	4	-	-	-	-	2	
Truck - ¼ton	2*	1	-	-	-	-	2	3	
Truck - small arms repair	-	-	1	-	-	-	-	-	
Truck - ¾ton Wpns Carrier	1**	-	3**	1	-	3**	1	2	* with .3cal MG
Truck - ¾ton Command	1	-	-	-	2	-	-	-	** with .5cal MG
Truck - compressor	-	-	-	-	-	-	-	-	
Truck - 2½ton cargo									
Ammunition	-	-	-	-	-	-	-	3**	note: Truck - small arms repair often 2½ton cargo truck fitted with workshop body
Combat	-	-	-	-	-	-	-	6**	
Gasoline & oil	-	-	-	-	-	-	-	3**	
Kitchen	-	-	-	-	-	-	-	5	
Maintenance	-	1**	-	-	-	-	2**	-	
Truck - 10ton Hvy Wrecker	-	-	-	-	-	-	1	-	
Trailer - 1ton cargo	-	-	-	-	-	-	-	17	

TANK DESTROYER BATTALION - VEHICLES - JUNE 1942

TO 18-27 & 18-28
 : 8th June 1942

	TANK DESTROYER COY (x3)								RECONNAISSANCE COY				
	Coy HQ		Lt TD Pln (x1)			Hy TD Pln x2 (ea)			Coy HQ		Pioneer Pln		3x Recce Plns (ea)
	HQ	Motor Maint	Pln HQ	2x Gun sect (ea)	AA	Pln HQ	2x Gun sect (ea)	AA	HQ	Motor Maint	Pln HQ	2x Pioneer sect (ea)	
Carriage, 37mm, SP (M6)	-	-	-	2	-	-	-	-	-	-	-	-	-
Carriage, 3-in, SP (M5)	-	-	-	-	-	-	2	-	-	-	-	-	-
GMC T1E4 (M13) .5cal AA MG	-	-	-	-	2	-	-	2	-	-	-	-	-
Car, Armored, Light, M3A1	2**	-	1**	-	-	1**	-	-	2**	-	1**	1**	2
Motorcycle - solo	2	-	-	-	-	-	-	-	3	-	-	-	2
Truck - ¼ton	2	1	5*[2]	-	-	5*[2]	-	-	1	1	-	-	6*[4]
Truck - small arms repair	-	-	-	-	-	-	-	-	-	-	-	-	-
Truck - ¾ton Wpns Carrier	-	-	1**	-	-	1**	-	-	-	-	-	1	-
Truck - ¾ton Command	-	-	-	-	-	-	-	-	-	-	-	-	-
Truck - compressor	-	-	-	-	-	-	-	-	-	-	1	-	-
Truck - 2½ton cargo													
Ammunition	-	-	-	-	-	-	-	-	-	-	-	-	-
Combat	-	-	-	-	-	-	-	-	-	-	-	-	-
Gasoline & oil	-	-	-	-	-	-	-	-	-	-	-	-	-
Kitchen	-	-	-	-	-	-	-	-	-	-	-	-	-
Maintenance	-	1**	-	-	-	-	-	-	-	1**	-	-	-
Truck - 10ton Hvy Wrecker	-	-	-	-	-	-	-	-	-	-	-	-	-
Trailer - 1ton cargo	-	-	-	-	-	-	-	-	-	-	-	2	-

TANK DESTROYER BATTALION (SP) - <u>VEHICLES</u> - <u>JANUARY 1943</u>

T/O & T/E 18-26 27th January 1943	HEADQUARTERS & HQ COMPANY								REMARKS
	Coy HQ		Comms Pln	Staff Pln			Maint Pln	Trans Pln	
	HQ Sec	Motor Maint		Admin	Intel	Supply			
Gun, 3-inch, ATk, SP, M10	-	-	-	-	-	-	-	-	Subs veh M3 75mm GMC
Car, Armd, Light, M3A1:									
Personnel	-	-	-	-	3**	-	-	-	Subs veh M2 half track
Recovery	-	-	-	-	-	-	-	-	rep by M32, October 1943
Reconnaissance	-	-	-	-	-	-	-	-	Subs veh M6 37mm GMC
Motorcycle, solo	-	-	4	-	-	-	-	-	
Armd Recovery Vehicle, M32	-	-	-	-	-	-	-	-	with 81mm mortar, Sub M31
Truck, Heavy Wrecker, 10ton	-	-	-	-	-	-	1	-	
Truck:									
¼ton 4x4 (jeep)	1*	-	-	-	-	-	-	2	
¾ton command	1	-	-	-	2	-	-	-	
¾ton weapons carrier	-	1*	2	-	-	2	1	-	
1½ton cargo	-	-	-	-	-	-	-	-	Subs veh M3 half track
1½ton CFM315 or CFM105	-	-	-	-	-	-	-	-	with compressor
2½ton cargo:									
Administration	-	-	-	1	-	-	-	-	
Ammunition	-	-	-	-	-	-	-	6**[1]	
Gasoline & oil	-	-	-	-	-	-	-	3**[1]	* with .3cal MG
Kitchen	-	-	-	-	-	-	-	5**[1]	** with .5cal MG
Maintenance	-	-	-	-	-	-	3**[1]	-	
Trailers:									
¼ton, 2whl, cargo	-	-	-	-	-	-	-	14	

TANK DESTROYER BATTALION (SP) - VEHICLES - JANUARY 1943

T/O & T/E 18-27 & 18-28 27th January 1943	TANK DESTROYER COMPANY (x3)				RECONNAISSANCE COMPANY				
	Coy HQ		3x TD Plns (ea)		Coy HQ		Pioneer Pln		3x Recce Plns (ea)
	HQ Sec	Motor Maint	Pln HQ	2x Gun sect (ea)	HQ Sec	Motor Maint	Pln HQ	2x Pioneer sect (ea)	
Gun, 3-inch, ATk, SP, M10	-	-	-	2**	-	-	-	-	-
Car, Armd, Light, M3A1:									
Personnel	2**	-	-	-	2**	-	1**	1**	-
Recovery	-	(1)	-	-	-	-	-	-	-
Reconnaissance	-	-	-	-	-	-	-	-	2
Motorcycle, solo	1	-	-	-	2	-	-	-	2
Armd Recovery Vehicle M32	-	(1)	-	-	-	-	-	-	-
Truck, Heavy Wrecker, 10ton	-	-	-	-	-	-	-	-	-
Truck:									
¼ton 4x4 (jeep)	1*	1	1*	-	1	-	-	-	4*
¾ton command	-	-	-	-	-	-	-	-	-
¾ton weapons carrier	-	-	-	-	-	1	-	-	-
1½ton cargo	-	-	1**	-	-	-	-	1**	-
1½ton CFM315 or CFM105	-	-	-	-	-	-	1	-	-
2½ton cargo:									
Administration	-	-	-	-	-	-	-	-	-
Ammunition	-	-	-	-	-	-	-	-	-
Gasoline & oil	-	-	-	-	-	-	-	-	-
Kitchen	-	-	-	-	-	-	-	-	-
Maintenance	-	1**	-	-	-	-	-	-	-
Trailers:									
¼ton, 2whl, cargo	-	-	1	-	-	-	-	-	-

TANK DESTROYER BATTALION (SP) - VEHICLES - MARCH 1944

T/O & E 18-25 15th March 1944	HEADQUARTERS & HQ COMPANY								REMARKS
	Coy HQ		Comms Pln	Staff Pln			Maint Pln	Trans Pln	
	HQ Sec	Motor Maint		Admin	Intel	Supply			
Carriage, Motor, Gun, 76mm	-	-	-	-	-	-	-	-	M10 or M18
Car, Armd, Light, M8, 37mm	-	-	-	-	-	-	-	-	subs veh M3A2 half track
Car, Armd, Utility, M20	-	-	-	-	3**	-	-	-	subs veh M3A2 half track
Armored Recovery Vehicle M32	-	-	-	-	-	-	-	-	carries 81mm mortar
Truck, Heavy Wrecker, M1	-	-	-	-	-	-	1	-	
Truck:									
¼ton 4x4 (jeep)	1*	-	2	-	3*[1]	1	1	-	
¾ton weapons carrier	1	1*	2	-	-	1	-	-	
1½ton 6x6 cargo	-	-	-	-	-	1	-	-	
1½ton CFM105	-	-	-	-	-	-	-	-	with compressor
2½ton cargo:									
Administration	-	-	-	1	-	-	-	-	
Ammunition	-	-	-	-	-	-	-	6	
Gasoline & oil	-	-	-	-	-	-	-	3 3**	
Kitchen	-	-	-	-	-	-	-	5	
Maintenance	-	-	-	-	-	-	3**[1]	-	
Trailers:									
¼ton, 2whl, cargo	-	1	-	-	-	-	-	-	
1ton, 2whl, cargo	-	-	-	1	-	1	2	14	
Ammunition, M10	-	-	-	-	-	-	-	-	

* with .3cal MG
** with .5cal MG

TANK DESTROYER BATTALION (SP) - VEHICLES - MARCH 1944

T/O & E 18-27 & 18-28 15th March 1944	TANK DESTROYER COMPANY (x3)				RECONNAISSANCE COMPANY				
	Coy HQ		3x TD Plns (ea)		Coy HQ		Pioneer Pln		3x Recce Plns (ea)
	HQ Sec	Motor Maint	Pln HQ	2x Gun sect (ea)	HQ Sec	Motor Maint	Pln HQ	2x Pioneer sect (ea)	
Carriage, Gun, Motor, 76mm	-	-	-	2**	-	-	-	-	-
Car, Armd, Light, M8, 37mm	-	-	-	-	-	-	-	-	*2**
Car, Armd, Utility, M20	2**	-	2**	-	2**	-	1**	-	-
Armored Recovery Vehicle M32	-	*1**	-	-	-	-	-	-	-
Truck, Heavy Wrecker, M1	-	-	-	-	-	-	-	-	-
Truck:									
¼ton 4x4 (jeep)	2*[1]	1	1*	-	2	1	-	-	5*[4]
¾ton weapons carrier	-	-	-	-	-	-	1	-	-
1½ton 6x6 cargo	-	-	-	-	-	-	-	2**	-
1½ton CFM105	-	-	-	-	-	-	1	-	-
2½ton cargo:									
Administration	-	-	-	-	-	-	-	-	-
Ammunition	-	-	-	-	-	-	-	-	-
Gasoline & oil	-	-	-	-	-	-	-	-	-
Kitchen	-	-	-	-	-	-	-	-	-
Maintenance	-	1**	-	-	-	-	-	-	-
Trailers:									
¼ton, 2whl, cargo	-	1	-	-	1	1	-	-	-
1ton, 2whl, cargo	-	-	-	-	1	-	-	-	-
Ammunition, M10	-	-	1	-	-	-	-	-	-

TANK DESTROYER BATTALION (SP) - VEHICLES - DECEMBER 1945

T/O & E 18-26 15th March 1944 (changes notice no.4 dated 5th Dec 1945)	HEADQUARTERS & HQ COMPANY								REMARKS Aircraft Section added T/O change of 12.45 Vehicles noted below
	Coy HQ		Comms Pln	Staff Pln			Maint Pln	Trans Pln	
	HQ Sec	Motor Maint		Admin	Intel	Supply			
Carriage, Gun, Motor, 90mm	-	-	-	-	-	-	-	-	M36, subs veh M18
Bulldozer, M1	-	-	-	-	-	-	-	-	M10/M36 conversion only
Car, Armd, Light, M8, 37mm	-	-	-	-	-	-	-	-	
Armd Utility Vehicle M39	-	-	-	-	3**[1]	-	-	-	from Dec 1945
Armored Recovery Vehicle M32	-	-	-	-	-	-	-	-	81mm mortar deleted 8.44
Truck, Heavy Wrecker, M1A1	-	-	-	-	-	-	1	-	replaced M1, Mar 1944
Truck:									
¼ton 4x4 (jeep)	1	-	2	-	3*[2]	-	-	2	+one to Aircraft Section
¼ton weapons carrier	1*	1	2	-	-	1	1	-	
1½ton 6x6 cargo	-	-	-	-	-	1	-	-	+one to Aircraft Section
1½ton CFM105	-	-	-	-	-	-	-	-	with compressor
2½ton cargo:									
Administration	-	-	-	1	-	-	-	-	
Ammunition	-	-	-	-	-	-	-	6	
Gasoline & oil	-	-	-	-	-	-	-	3 **[3]	
Kitchen	-	-	-	-	-	-	-	5	
Maintenance	-	-	-	-	-	-	3**[1]	-	
Trailers:									
¼ton, 2whl, cargo	-	1	-	-	-	-	-	-	+one to Aircraft Section
1ton, 2whl, cargo	-	-	-	1	-	1	2	8	
Ammunition, M10	-	-	-	-	-	-	-	6	rep 1ton trailer Aug 1944
250 gallon, water	1	-	-	-	-	-	-	-	
Aircraft, liaison	-	-	-	-	-	-	-	-	+two to Aircraft Section

Remarks box:
* with .3cal MG
** with .5cal MG

TANK DESTROYER BATTALION (SP) - VEHICLES - DECEMBER 1945

T/O & E 18-27 & 18-28 15th March 1944 (changes notice nos.5 dated 5th Dec 1945)	TANK DESTROYER COMPANY (x3)				RECONNAISSANCE COMPANY				
	Coy HQ		3x TD Plns (ea)		Coy HQ		Pioneer Pln		3x Recce Plns (ea)
	HQ Sec	Motor Maint	Pln HQ	2x Gun sect (ea)	HQ Sec	Motor Maint	Pln HQ	2x Pioneer sect (ea)	
Carriage, Gun, Motor, 90mm	-	-	-	2**	-	-	-	-	-
Bulldozer, M1	2	-	-	-	-	-	-	-	-
Car, Armd, Light, M8, 37mm	-	-	-	-	-	-	-	-	*2**
Armd Utility Vehicle M39	2	-	2	-	2	-	1	-	-
Armored Recovery Vehicle M32	-	1	-	-	-	-	-	-	-
Truck, Heavy Wrecker, M1A1	-	-	-	-	-	-	-	-	-
Truck:									
¼ton 4x4 (jeep)	2*[1]	1	1*	-	2	1	-	-	5*[4]
¾ton weapons carrier	-	-	-	-	-	1	-	-	-
1½ton 6x6 cargo	-	-	-	-	-	-	-	2**	-
1½ton CFM105	-	-	-	-	1	-	-	-	-
2½ton cargo:									
Administration	-	-	-	-	-	-	-	-	-
Ammunition	-	-	-	-	-	-	-	-	-
Gasoline & oil	-	-	-	-	-	-	-	-	-
Kitchen	-	-	-	-	-	-	-	-	-
Maintenance	-	1**	-	-	-	-	-	-	-
Trailers:									
¼ton, 2whl, cargo	-	1	-	-	1	1	-	-	-
1ton, 2whl, cargo	-	-	-	-	-	-	-	-	-
Ammunition, M10	-	-	1	-	-	-	-	-	-
250 gallon, water	1	-	-	-	1	-	-	-	-
Aircraft, liaison	-	-	-	-	-	-	-	-	-

TANK DESTROYER BATTALION (TOWED) - VEHICLES - MAY 1943

TO 18-36 : 7th May 1943	HEADQUARTERS & HQ COY								REMARKS
	Coy HQ	2x Recce Plns (ea)	Comms Pln	Staff Pln			Maint Pln	Transp Pln	
				Adm	Int	Sup			
Gun, 3in, ATk, towed, M1	-	-	-	-	-	-	-	-	
Car, Armd, Light, M8	-	2	-	-	-	-	-	-	Subs veh half-track M2
Car, Armd, Utility, M10+	1**	-	-	-	3**	-	-	-	Subs veh half-track M2
Half-Track, Personnel, M3	-	-	-	-	-	-	-	-	
Motorcycle, solo	-	2	4	-	-	-	-	-	
Truck - ¼ton	1	4*	-	-	-	-	1	2	
Truck - ¾ton, command	1	-	-	-	-	2	-	-	
Truck - ¾ton, wpns carrier	-	-	2	-	-	2	1	-	
Truck - 1½ton, 6x6 cargo	-	-	-	-	-	-	-	-	Subs veh half-track M3
Truck - 2½ton, cargo									
Administrative	-	-	-	1	-	-	-	-	
Ammunition	-	-	-	-	-	-	-	*6**	1x .3cal, 2x .5cal MG (total)
Kitchen	-	-	-	-	-	-	-	*4**	1x .3cal 1x .5cal MG (total)
Maintenance	-	-	-	-	-	-	2**	-	1x .5cal MG (total)
Truck, Heavy Wrecker, M1	-	-	-	-	-	-	1*	-	
Trailer - 2whl, 1ton	-	-	-	-	-	-	2	10	

> * armed with .3cal MG
> ** armed with .5cal MG

+ the M10 armd utility was later designated 'M20' to avoid confusion with the M10 GMC

TANK DESTROYER BATTALION (TOWED) - VEHICLES - MAY 1943

ATTACHED MEDIC COY - SP & TOWED TD BNS

TO 18-37 : 7th May 1943	TANK DESTROYER COY (x3)			
	Coy HQ		3x TD Plns (ea)	
	HQ Sec	Motor Maint	Pln HQ	2x Gun sects (ea)
Gun, 3in, ATk, towed, M1	-	-	-	2
Car, Armd, Light, M8	-	-	-	-
Car, Armd, Utility, M10	2**	-	-	-
Half-Track, Personnel, M3	-	-	-	1*, 1**
Motorcycle, solo	1	-	-	-
Truck - ¼ton	1*	1	4 *2	-
Truck - ¾ton, command	-	-	-	-
Truck - ¾ton, wpns carrier	-	-	-	-
Truck - 1½ton, 6x6 cargo	-	-	1	-
Truck - 2½ton, cargo				
Administrative	-	-	-	-
Ammunition	-	-	-	-
Kitchen	-	-	-	-
Maintenance	1**	-	-	-
Truck - Heavy Wrecker, M1	-	-	-	-
Trailer - 2whl, 1ton	-	-	1	-

TO & E 18-25 : 15th March 1944 TO & E 18-35 : 1st September 1944	MEDIC COY (SP & TOWED BNS)
Captain First lieutenant (or)	1
Staff sergeant	1
Corporal	1
other ranks*	13
Truck - ¼ton	4
Truck - 1½ton, 6x6 cargo	1
Trailer - 2whl, 1ton	1

* includes Company Aid Men,
  2 per TD Coy, 2 per Recce Coy

1x ¾ton ambulance added to Medic
Coys attached to SP Bns, 12.44

TANK DESTROYER BATTALION (TOWED) - VEHICLES - SEPTEMBER 1944

TO & E 18-36 : 1st September 1944	HEADQUARTERS & HQ COY								REMARKS
	Coy HQ	2x Recce Plns (ea)	Comms Pln	Staff Pln			Maint Pln	Transp Pln	Staff Platoon sections Administrative Intelligence & Operations Supply
				Adm	Int	Sup			
Gun, 3in, ATk, towed,	-	-	-	-	-	-	-	-	
Car, Armd, Light, (M8)	-	2	-	-	-	-	-	-	
Car, Armd, Utility, (M20)	-	-	-	-	4**	-	-	-	Subs veh Half-Track M3
Veh, Armd, Utility, (M39)	-	-	-	-	-	-	-	-	
Truck - ¼ton	1	5*	2	-	3	-	-	2	* armed with .3cal MG
Truck - ¾ton, wpns carrier	2	-	2	-	-	1	1	-	** armed with .5calMG
Truck - 1½ton 6x6 cargo	-	-	-	-	-	1	-	-	
Truck - 2½ton, cargo									
Administrative	-	-	-	1	-	-	-	-	
Ammunition	-	-	-	-	-	-	-	6⌐	
Kitchen	-	-	-	-	-	-	-	4⌐ 4**	
Maintenance	-	-	-	-	-	-	3	-	
Truck - Heavy Wrecker	-	-	-	-	-	-	1*	-	
Trailer - 2whl, ¼ton	-	-	1	-	-	-	-	-	
Trailer - 2whl, 1ton	-	-	-	1	-	1	2	4	
Trailer - ammunition, M10	-	-	-	-	-	-	-	6	

Note : No further organisational changes. Towed units commenced conversion to SP units, only six towed
battalions remaining in May 1945

TANK DESTROYER BATTALION (TOWED) - VEHICLES - SEPT 1944

TO & E 18-37
: 1st September 1944

| | TANK DESTROYER COY (x3) | | | |
| | Coy HQ | | 3x TD Plns (ea) | |
	HQ Sec	Motor Maint	Pln HQ	2x Gun sects (ea)
Gun, 3in, ATk, towed	-	-	-	2
Car, Armd, Light (M8)	-	-	-	-
Car, Armd, Utility (M20)	2**	-	-	-
Veh, Armd, Utility (M39)	-	-	-	2**
Truck - $\frac{1}{4}$ton	2*[1]	1	4*[2]	-
Truck - $\frac{3}{4}$ton wpns carrier	-	-	-	-
Truck - 1$\frac{1}{2}$ton 6x6 cargo	-	-	1	-
Truck - 2$\frac{1}{2}$ton cargo				
Administrative	-	-	-	-
Ammunition	-	-	-	-
Kitchen	-	-	-	-
Maintenance	-	1**	-	-
Truck - Heavy Wrecker	-	-	-	-
Trailer - 2whl, $\frac{1}{4}$ton	-	1	-	-
Trailer - 2whl, 1ton	-	-	-	-
Trailer - ammunition, M10	-	-	-	-

NOTES ON ITEMS OF VEHICLE EQUIPMENT

Individual tools carried on each truck include:

> Axe (4lb), Pickmattock (5lb) Shovel, 18-in Machete, canvas water bucket.

Towing : towrope 20ft x 1-in dia for $\frac{1}{4}$ton and $\frac{3}{4}$ton trucks

> towchain 16ft x 7/16-in dia for 1$\frac{1}{2}$ton & 2$\frac{1}{2}$ton trucks

Camouflage: Cotton netting as follows:

> 22ft x 22ft for $\frac{1}{4}$ton truck and $\frac{1}{4}$ton trailer
> 29ft x 29ft for $\frac{3}{4}$ton truck 1ton & M10 trailers
> 36ft x 44ft for 1$\frac{1}{2}$ton, 2$\frac{1}{2}$ton, heavy wrecker trucks and M20/M39 utilities

> Twine netting as follows

> 15ft x 15ft for dismounted .5cal machine guns

Gasoline drums, with handle, 5gals

> 1 per $\frac{1}{4}$ton truck
> 2 per $\frac{3}{4}$ton, 1$\frac{1}{2}$ton, 2$\frac{1}{2}$ton trucks
> 4 per heavy wrecker
> 170 per load carrying 2$\frac{1}{2}$ton truck

RADIO COMMUNICATIONS EQUIPMENT

Types of set :
    SR (Short Range)   models SCR808/SCR608/SCR610 vehicle sets, range 5 miles, voice only, push-button transmitter/receiver, 120 crystals on 27-39mc

    MR (Med Range)   models SCR193/SCR245 generally superceded by SCR506, range 25 miles +, std veh. set, 4 crystal-controlled frequencies, continuous wave and voice.

    PS (Panel set)   model AP-50-A, believed to be short range set fitted to veh. instrument panel

    Interphone   model RC-99, believed to be standard inter-crew communication in AFV's

---

TYPICAL DISTRIBUTION - June 1942 (model not specified in T/O & E)

Vehicle Type	HQ Company	Gun Company	Recce Company
M3A1 Recce Vehicle or M2 Half-Track	4 sets	5 sets	7 sets
Truck - ¾ton Command	3 sets	none	none
Truck - ¾ton Wpns Carrier	2 sets	none	none
Truck - ¼ton (jeep)	3 sets	none	19 sets

TYPICAL DISTRIBUTION - March 1944 (SP Unit)

Vehicle Type	HQ Company	Gun Company	Recce Company
M20 Armd Utility	3x SR, 2x MR, 1x PS	8x SR, 6x PS	3x SR, 1x MR
M8 Armored Car	none	none	6x SR, 6x PS
M10, M18 GMC	none	12x SR, 12x Int, 12x PS	none
M32 Armd Recovery Veh.	none	1x SR, 1x Int, 1x PS	none
Truck - ¼ton (jeep)	4x SR	1x SR	13x SR
Truck - ¾ton Wpns Carrier	3x SR, 1x MR	none	1x SR
Truck - 1½ton cargo	1x SR	none	2x SR

note, in addition to the above, four trucks (type unspecified) were fitted with the AP-50-A Panel Set

VEHICLE MARKINGS

National Identification

In common with other units, the white star was the predominant marking, point to rear on horizontal surfaces and upward on vertical surfaces. Tank destroyers were not included as a seperate group in the 1942 marking regulations, and it is assumed that the markings applicable to the nearest vehicle type were adopted (Dodge 4x4, M3 half-track or medium tank). In N.Africa the star might be superimposed on a blue disc, particularly when light vehicle tones were employed on camouflage. From Sicily onwards, a white circum-circle was added to aid air recognition, usually on horizontal surfaces. Tank destroyers were named as a seperate group in the 1945 regulations. Star diameter in inches is indicated below:-

	Dodge 4x4	half-track		med.tank	Tank Destroyer
F. bumper center	6	-	Turret rear	20	-
Radiator center	-	20	Turret sides	20	-
Center of sides	10	20	Turret top	20	-
Center of rear	-	15	Hull sides	-	20
Bonnet top	-	36	Hull rear	-	20
			Engine deck	36	45

Vehicle Serial Numbers

Numbers were prefixed by the national identification 'US', 'USA' or 'US ARMY' followed by the letter 'W' for 'War Department'. The first two numerals denoted the vehicle type, the remainder the individual vehicle number. Prefix '60' was used for the M6 vehicles and '40' for all other tracked and half-tracked GMC's. The suffix 'S' was used to identify radio suppressed vehicles.

Bridge Classification Numbers

Similar to the British system, the bridge classification number was displayed in black on a yellow disc situated at the front of the vehicle. Classifications included '2' for the M6 GMC, '8' for half-tracks, '18' for the M18 and '30' for the M10/M36 series. When towing, the weight of the tractor and trailer combined would be displayed over the weight of the towing vehicle alone (weight approximating to bridge code). The code for an M3 half-track towing a 3-inch gun was probably 10 over 8.

VEHICLE TACTICAL MARKINGS - BUMPER CODES

Official marking system for the identification of the command and arm-of-service of vehicles

ARMY	Code	BN	Code
1st	1A	612	612TD
3rd	3A	601	601TD
5th	5A		etc..
7th	7A		
9th	9A		

COY	Code	PLATOON	Vehicle No.
HQ	HQ	(Coy HQ)	1 - 10
A	A	1st	11 - 20
B	B	2nd	21 - 30
C	C	3rd	31 - 40
Recce	R	4th	41 - 50

Positioning of Bumper Code

Bumper Codes - examples

1A 629TD	A18	= 1st Army, 629th TD Bn, A Coy, 18th vehicle
7A 636TD	HQ31	= 7th Army, 636th TD Bn, HQ Coy, 31st vehicle
9A 628TD	R14	= 9th Army, 628th TD Bn, Recce Coy, 14th vehicle
5A 701TD	C27	= 5th Army, 701st TD Bn, C Coy, 27th vehicle

Alternative displays

In some cases, the company and vehicle code was displayed on the hull side in large white letters or on the rear of the turret counter weight. The 601st Bn used a Battalion insignia of red 'Y' on yellow square with the coy no at the lower left corner.

BUMPER CODES - ARMY COMMANDS

	11.42	1.43	5.43	7.43	9.43	11.43	1.44	2.44	5.44	8.44	10.44	3.45	4.45
5th ARMY	601	601	601	601*	601	601	601	601	601	701	701	679	701
	701	701	701	701	636	636	636	636	636	776	804	701	804
			776	776	645	645	645	645	645	804	805	804	805
			813	813	701	701	701	701	701	805	894	805	894
			894	894	771	776	776	776	776	894		894	
			899	899	776	805	805	805	805				
					813	813	894	894	894				
					894	894							
					899	899							

* attached to 7th ARMY for operations in Sicily

BUMPER CODES - ARMY COMMANDS

	1944							1945				
	June	July	Aug	Sept	Oct	Nov	Dec	Jan	Feb	Mar	Apr	May
1st ARMY	607 801 612 803 635 821 644 823 702 899	612 801 630 803 634 818 635 821 654 823 702 893 703 899	612 703 629 705 630 801 634 803 635 823 654 893 702 899	628 702 629 703 630 741 634 801 635 823 645 893	601 645 628 692 629 693 634 801 636 893	612 801 628 802 629 803 634 811 644 820 692 893	612 703 628 772 629 801 634 814 643 817 644 820 692 823	612 772 628 801 629 814 634 820 638 823 643 893	612 661 630 692 634 703 644 814 648 893 656 899	612 661 630 692 634 703 644 814 648 893	612 703 634 803 644 807 648 814 656 817 661 893	602 661 605 814 612 817 633 893
3rd ARMY		607 803 644 813 802	607 802 610 813 612 814 628 818 654	607 774 610 807 654 808 691 814 773 818	602 704 607 705 609 773 610 774 638 808 654 818 691	602 705 607 773 609 774 610 803 614 808 654 818 691	602 773 607 774 609 802 610 803 654 807 691 808 704 811 705 818	602 704 607 773 609 774 610 802 611 803 631 811 654 818 691	602 773 607 774 609 802 610 803 691 808 704 811 705 818	602 774 607 803 691 808 704 811 705 818 773	602 705 603 773 607 808 635 811 691 818 704 820	607 705 610 773 634 803 635 808 656 811 691 818 704 820
7th ARMY			601 645 636	601 636	776 813	601 776 636 813 645 824	601 813 636 824 645 827 776	601 776 630 807 636 813 645 824 654 825 705 827	601 801 614 807 636 813 645 822 772 824 776 827	601 648 609 692 610 776 614 807 635 813 636 822 645 824	601 692 609 776 610 801 614 822 636 824 645	601 776 609 807 614 813 636 822 692 824
9th ARMY				612 705 644 802	612 811 644 814 802 823 807 893	814 823	638	628 771 644 817 692 893	605 702 628 771 629 802 638 809 643 817 654 823	605 691 628 702 629 771 638 772 643 802 645 809 654 823	605 771 628 772 629 801 638 802 643 809 654 823 702	628 702 629 703 638 771 643 772 644 801 645 809 654 823

N.B.   Examples only, not to be considered as a complete inventory
Outside continental USA, it is believed that only the 'Army' number appeared with the TD unit number.

INDEX TO TABLES OF ORGANISATION & EQUIPMENT - TANK DESTROYERS

BIBLIOGRAPHY

U.S. War Department	Tables of Organisation & Equipment	National Archives (Reference Branch), Washington & Department of the Army, (Center of Military History)
Chamberlain P. & Ellis C.	British & American Tanks of World War II	Arms & Armour Press
Church, J.	Military Vehicles of World War II	New Orchard Editions
Forty, G.	U.S. Army Handbook 1939-45	Ian Allen Ltd
Gabel, Dr C.R.	Seek, Strike & Destroy: U.S. Army Tank Destroyer Doctrine in World War Two (Leavington Paper No.12)	Combat Studies Institute, U.S. Army Command & General Staff College, Fort Leavenworth, Kansas.
Madej, V.W.	U.S. Army Order of Battle: Europe	Game Publishing
Madej, V.W.	U.S. Army Order of Battle: Mediterranean & Europe 1942-45	Game Publishing
Stanton, S.	U.S. Orders of Battle	
Wise, T.	World War II Military Vehicle Markings	Patrick Stephens Limited
Zaloga, S.J.	US Tank Destroyers of World War II	Arms & Armour Press
Zaloga, S.J.	US Half-Tracks of World War II	Osprey Vanguard

ACKNOWLEDGEMENTS

The author wishes to acknowledge the help and encouragement received from many people during the preparation of this book, in particular Messrs David Fletcher, Ewen Bayley, Patrice Debucquoy, John Wilkes, Leo J. Daugherty III and the staff of the National Archives and Center of Military History who dealt patiently with my enquiries. Not least, my thanks to the readers of the Datafile Series for their support and comments.

Towed 37mm with
¼ ton truck
(1:72 scale Hasegawa)

(Author)

M36 90mm GMC
(1:76 scale Fujimi)

(Author)

THE DATAFILE SERIES

DATAFILE 1 (2nd Edition)
'British Tanks & Formations 1939-45'
ISBN 0 9512126 2 1

DATAFILE 2
'Divisions of the British Army 1939-45'
ISBN 0 9512126 0 5

DATAFILE 3
'Brigades of the British Army 1939-45'
ISBN 0 9512126 1 3

DATAFILE 4
'German Tanks & Formations 1939-45'
ISBN 0 9512126 4 8

DATAFILE 5
'British Armoured & Infantry Regiments
1939-45'
ISBN 0 9512126 3 X

DATAFILE 6
'U.S. Divisions - N.Africa & Europe 1942-45'
ISBN 0 9512126 5 6

DATAFILE 7
'U.S. Tank Destroyers of World War Two'
ISBN 0 9512126 6 4